TESTIMONY

ACKNOWLEDGEMENTS

Many thanks to Ann and Peter Sansom who published my
first book of Lipkin versions, *After Semyon Izrailevich Lipkin*
(Smith|Doorstop, 2011) and to the Poetry Book Society for
commending that volume.

ALSO BY YVONNE GREEN

A Close Reading of 53 poems by Semyon Izrailevich Lipkin
(Hendon Press, 2023)
Jam & Jerusalem (Smith|Doorstop, 2018)
Honoured (Smith|Doorstop, 2015)
Selected Poems and Translations (Smith|Doorstop, 2014)
After Semyon Izrailevich Lipkin (Smith|Doorstop, 2011)
The Assay (Smith|Doorstop, 2010)
Boukhara (Smith|Doorstop, 2008)

Anthologies

The Penguin Book of Russian Poetry (Penguin, 2015)
Russia is Burning – Poems of the Great Patriotic War (Hachette,
2020)
Mapping Faith: Theologies of Migration and Community (Jessica
Kingsley, 2020)
Resistance – Voices of Exiled Writers (Palewell Press, 2020)

HENDON
PRESS

TESTIMONY
FROM THE LITERARY MEMOIRS
OF SEMYON IZRAILEVICH LIPKIN
(1911−2003)

Translated by Yvonne Green
and Sergei Makarov

With an introduction by
Professor Donald Rayfield

Published 2023 by
Hendon Press
2I Wykeham Road,
Hendon,
London
NW4 2TB

ISBN 978-1-739778-51-4

British Library Cataloguing-in-Publication Data.
A catalogue record for this book is available from the
British Library.

Designed & Typeset by Utter

CONTENTS

In memory of Inna Lisnyanskaya (1928 – 2014)

CHRONOLOGY OF HISTORICAL EVENTS DURING LIPKIN'S LIFE

1911, September 6 (Julian Calendar)
    Semyon Izrailevich Lipkin born 19 September 1911 (Gregorian Calendar), Odesa; son of Israel and Rosalia Lipkin; his father had a tailoring business.

1914, June 28
    Franz Ferdinand, Archduke of Austria and his wife are assassinated in Sarajevo by Gavrilo Princip, the *casus belli* of the First World War.

1917   Bolshevik revolution.

1918–20   Civil war.

1921–22   Famine in Volga basin

1924   Death of Lenin. Petrograd is renamed Leningrad. Stalin begins to take over power.

1925   Lipkin's first poem published, age 15. Eduard Bagritsky recognises the merit of this first publication.

1930, February
    Central Committee Decree calls for the liquidation of the Kulaks as a class.

April 14   Mayakovsky commits suicide.

1931   Stalin orders enforced collectivization. Kalmyk Buddhist monasteries closed, and religious texts burned.

1932   Independent literary groups closed, and Union of Soviet Writers formed.

1932–34   Between eight and ten million peasants killed by their own government's Terror Famine (*Holodomor*) in Ukraine, Volga basin, Kalmyk ASSR and elsewhere in the Soviet Union. Shostakovich's *Lady Macbeth of*

Mtsensk denounced.

1936–38 Approximately half the members of the Soviet political, military and intellectual elite are imprisoned or shot. Around 380,000 supposed 'Kulaks' are killed, as are around 250,000 members of various national minorities.

1937 Lipkin graduates from the Moscow Economics Engineering Institute. While studying engineering he had begun studying Farsi, followed by other Oriental languages including Dagestani, Kalmyk, Kyrgyz, Tatar, Tajik, Uzbek, Kabardian, Yiddish and Moldavian; also their history and culture including Islam and Buddhism.

1939–41 Death of 70,000 mentally handicapped Germans in the Nazis' euthanasia programme.

1939 Nazi-Soviet pact. Beginning of Second World War.

1941 Germany invades the Soviet Union. Leningrad is blockaded and Moscow under threat. Two and half million Polish Jews are gassed in Chelmno, Majdanek, Belzec, Sobibor, Treblinka and Auschwitz. Lipkin's friend, Vasily Grossman, starts work as a war correspondent for *Red Star* (*Krasnaya Zvezda* – the Red Army newspaper).

1941–42 Two million Jews are shot in western areas of the Soviet Union; Grossman's mother is one of the approximately twelve thousand Jews killed in a single day at the airport outside Berdichev.

1941–45 Lipkin served in the Red Army, including at Stalingrad.

1941, September 8
Siege of Stalingrad begins.

1942–1943, August to February
Battle of Stalingrad.

1942, December
Soviets reconquer the Kalmyk ASSR.

1943, July/August
Decisive Soviet victory at the Battle of Kursk.

1943   Stalin declares all Kalmyks to be Nazi collaborators. In December the total population of the Kalmyk ASSR, including communists, is deported to prison camps in Siberia and Central Asia.

1944, January 27
Siege of Stalingrad lifted.

1944, April–June
436,000 Hungarian Jews are gassed at Auschwitz, in only fifty-six days.

1944, August–October
Warsaw uprising.

1945, January 27
Liberation of Auschwitz.

1945, May 9
Surrender of Germany.

1946   Nuremberg Trial of the Nazi leadership. In the Soviet Union, Andrey Zhdanov tightens control over the arts.

1948   Murder of Solomon Mikhoels, head of the Jewish Anti-Fascist Committee, which was then dissolved. The plates for the Soviet edition of *The Black Book*, a documentary of the Final Solution in the Soviet Union and Poland, compiled by Ilya Ehrenburg and Grossman between 1943–1946 were destroyed.

1953   Publication of article in *Pravda* in January about the Jewish "Killer Doctors." Preparations continue for Stalin's purge of Soviet Jews. March 5: Death of

Stalin. April 4: Official acknowledgement that the case against the 'Killer Doctors' is fabricated.

1956, February
Nikita Khrushchev's Secret Speech to the Communist Party. He denounces the forcible exile of the Kalmyks, Karachai, Chechen, Ingush, and Balkhars.

1956, Oct–Nov
Suppression of Hungarian insurrection.

1957   Some Kalmyks allowed to return.

1958   The former Kalmyk ASSR reconstituted. Boris Pasternak's *Dr Zhivago* is published abroad. Under pressure from the Soviet authorities he declines the Nobel Prize.

1960, October
Against the advice of Yekaterina Vasilievna Zabolotskaya and Lipkin, Vasily Grossman submits his novel *Life and Fate* for publication to the editors of *Znamya*.

1961   The KGB raid Grossman's home and destroy all the copies of *Life and Fate* they can. Lipkin keeps one copy at Peredelkino and later transfers it to Sergei and Lena Makarov's attic in Moscow for safe keeping. Unbeknown to Lipkin, Lyola Klestova has been given the original manuscript by Grossman who arranges prior to his death for her to give her copy to Vyacheslav Loboda.

1962, November
Alexander Solzhenitsyn's *One Day in the Life of Ivan Denisovich* published in the Soviet Union.

1964   Fall of Khrushchev; death of Vasily Grossman.

1966   Trial of Andrei Sinyavski and Yuli Daniel.

1967   Lipkin receives the Rudaki State Prize of the Tadzhik

SSR. Lipkin's first collection of poetry *Ochevidets* [*Eyewitness*] published. His poem 'Conjunction' is read as coded support for Israel.

1968, August
　　　　　Warsaw Pact invasion of Czechoslovakia.

1968　　　Lipkin made People's Poet of the Kalmyk ASSR.

1970　　　First issue of Jewish samizdat journal *Exodus*. Lipkin's *A Notebook of Being* published.

1971　　　Beginning of permitted Jewish emigration.

1973　　　Solzhenitsyn's *Gulag Archipelago* published in Paris.

1974　　　Solzhenitsyn exiled from the USSR.

1975　　　Andrei Sakharov awarded Nobel Peace Prize. Lipkin's *Vechnyi Den'* [*Eternal Day*] published. Lipkin asks the writer Vladamir Voinovich to help him get his copy of *Life and Fate* (the manuscript) published in the West. Voinovich inexpertly microfilms the manuscript but then gets Sakharov to make a better microfilm. The latter film reaches the Parisian dissident journal *Kontinent* via Russia's Austrian attaché. Only extracts are published.

1977　　　Voinovich microfilms the manuscript again and it reaches Yefim Etkind and Shimon Markish via the Austrian Professor Rosemary Zeigler.

1979　　　Lipkin and Inna Lisnyanskaya submit their poetry to the anthology, *Metropol*, which is rejected by the Soviet authorities.

1980　　　Lipkin resigns from the Union of Writers. Internal exile of Sakharov. Grossman's *Life and Fate* published in Switzerland, from Voinovich's films of the manuscript as painstakingly collated by Etkin and Markish.

1981　　　*Metropol* published in the United States. Lipkin's *Volya*

[*Free Will*] published in Russian in the US on the initiative of Joseph Brodsky.

1982   Death of Leonid Brezhnev.

1984   Death of Yuri Andropov. Lipkin's *Kochevi Onon'* [*A Nomadic Flame*] published in Russian in US.

1985   Mikhail Gorbachev becomes general secretary of the Communist Party of the Soviet Union. The period known as Perestroika begins. Loboda's widow shows the original manuscript of *Life and Fate* to Fyodor Guber and it was used to correct textual lacunae in the Swiss version before *Life and Fate* was first published in Moscow. The first publication in Russia of *Life and Fate* along with Grossman's *Everything Flows* and important works by Sigizmund Krzhizhanovsky, Andrey Platonov, Varlam Shalamov, Solzhenitsyn and many others.

1986   Lipkin's *Kartiny i golosa* [*Pictures and Voices*] published in Russian in London. Lipkin is reinstated into the Writers' Union.

1988   Pasternak's *Doctor Zhivago* published in Soviet Union. October: Gorbachev becomes president.

1989, November
        Fall of Berlin Wall.

1991   Dissolution of USSR. Lipkin awarded Tukai Prize. His *Lunnyi Svet* [*Moonlight*] and *Pis'mena* [*Letters*] are published.

1992   Outbreak of civil war in Tajikistan.

1993   Boris Yeltsin suppresses armed rising by Supreme Soviet.

1995   Lipkin awarded the Sakharov Prize by the European Parliament, and the Pushkin Prize by the Alfred Toepfer Foundation, Germany.

1997   Lipkin's *Posokh* [*Shepherd's Crook*] published.

2000   Putin elected president. Lipkin's *Sem' desiatiletii* [*Seven Decades*] published.

2003, May 31
            Death of Semyon Izrailevich Lipkin at Peredelkino.

PREFACE

For the last fifteen years I have translated the poems of Semyon Izrailevich Lipkin (1911–2003) and his widow Inna Lisnyanskaya (1928–2014) using literal versions provided by their son-in-law, the writer and historian, Sergei Makarov. This book constitutes translations of extracts from the second edition of Lipkin's memoirs *Kvadriga* [*Testimony*], dealing with Anna Akhmatova, Marina Tsvetaeva (whom Lipkin met publically when most felt it safer not to) and Vasily Grossman among others. *Kvadriga* has been widely quoted by many literary historians of the period and Robert Chandler, who generously contributed an appendix translating a short extract of this memoir to my initial book of translations of Lipkin's poems, *After Semyon Izrailevich Lipkin* (Smith|Doorstop, 2011), prefaced that extract with a wish to see the whole of Lipkin's memoir translated in the future which set me on my way.

The section dealing with Grossman contains passages which do not appear in current translations or Russian editions. On 25th July 2013 Russia's Federal Security Service, the KGB's successors, released Grossman's manuscripts and supporting documents which they had seized in 1961 so academics will in due course have an opportunity to form a view on the entirety of Grossman's drafts[1]. Lipkin describes Grossman both reading the work in progress to him and leaving a manuscript copy with him which he hid from the KGB in Sergei and Lena Makarov's flat. He later gave this to his wife, Inna Lisnyanskaya, to take to Vladimir Voinovich, once he'd agreed to help Lipkin in initiating its publication in the West.

I first came to know Lipkin's work as a result of Daniel Weissbort's translations of Lisnyanskaya's poems (*Far From Sodom*, Arc Publications, 2005). Weissbort and Valentina

---

1   http://sputniknews.com/russia/20130725/182420636.html

Polukhina introduced me to Lisnyanskaya who, until her death in 2014, was a great friend and source of encouragement. Lisnyanskaya's daughter, Lena Makarova, gave me generous and patient support from the outset. Lena works tirelessly documenting the thousands of lectures, plays, operas, concerts, and works of fine art produced at Terezin by inmates who went on to their deaths. Every moment she gave me was beyond value.

Lipkin couldn't publish his huge œuvre until his seventh decade. In the interim he translated the literatures of cultures which Stalin intended to obliterate, becoming a repository of their idiom, culture and history for which he was recognized after Perestroika. The translators' footnotes (marked with a +), the chronology, and the appendices to this volume are intended to furnish a sense of the enormity of his linguistic and intellectual reach. Lipkin's own footnotes have been marked with an *.

I'm indebted to Sharon Dewinter and Gila Pfeffer for their comments on my drafts, to Abigail Hayton for our discussions on this project and for her Suggested Further Reading, to Keith Lauchlan for editorial work, design and typesetting, and to countless other friends for their encouragement.

Yvonne Green
February 2023
London

INTRODUCTION

Lipkin and Lisnyanskaya

Semyon Lipkin (1911–2003) and his wife Inna Lisnyanskaya (1928–2014) formed one of the most extraordinary couples in the history of Russian literature. As poets they never achieved the same international (or national) recognition as the greatest of their contemporaries – Pasternak, Tsvetaeva, Akhmatova, and Mandelstam – for they worked within existing traditions, rather than trying to break the mould. But as witnesses to the struggles of their contemporaries and to the fortunes of Russia under Stalin's terror, Nazi invasion and the post-Stalinist period of lies and suppression, Lipkin and Lisnyanskaya deserve the rank of martyrs, even though they were both vouchsafed a longevity extraordinary for a Russian poet in any era.

No Russian poet has written poetry over such a long period as Lipkin: his first poem appeared in 1926 when he was 15, his last shortly before his death in 2003. The thousand or so poems he wrote over those seventy-five years are all beautifully crafted, thoughtful and original. If he has never been ranked with Osip Mandelstam and Marina Tsvetaeva (both of whom patronised him, and were helped by him), it is because he deliberately aligned himself with poets such as Ivan Bunin: craftsmen, not magi; silver, rather than gold. Under Stalin, Lipkin remained, by some miracle, an honest intellectual and an observant Jew, seeking neither approval nor martyrdom. He was also an Orientalist, most admired as a translator of the Kyrgyz national epic, a modest career that became dangerous when Stalin in the late 1930s changed official encouragement of such national epics to condemnation of their 'nationalist' deviations. In the late 1920s, official Soviet policy encouraged the popularization of the culture of national minorities; under the Great Terror of 1937–8 such popularization suddenly became the crime of bourgeois nationalism. And towards the end of the Second World War, in many cases, when a national minority, such as the Kalmyks or Crimean Tatars, had hoped for liberation by Hitler from Soviet rule, it became outright treason. Lipkin, unlike many translators of languages such as Kyrgyz, had a genuine competence in Central Asian Turkic: his gifts became a source of jeopardy, nearly as dangerous as his Jewishness, once Stalin took the anti-semitic mantle over from Hitler.

After the fall of the USSR, Lipkin became better known. But his most widely read work has been not his verse but his *Kvadriga*, memoirs of his extraordinarily long and wide-ranging friendships: their humour and observation offset only by a certain puritanism. Nevertheless, Lipkin often reminds one of James Boswell: his visits to Akhmatova and his long friendship with Vasily Grossman are recorded with the same remarkable talent for verbatim recall and for unjudgemental self-effacement. Like Boswell, Lipkin was pleased by any words of praise he received from his idols. Like Boswell, Lipkin played a vital role in immortalizing his collocutor. It is quite possible that, had Lipkin and Lisnyanskaya not succeeded in preserving a manuscript of Grossman's novel *Life and Fate* – arguably the most important work of fiction in twentieth-century Russia – it would have vanished into the cellars of the KGB.

Lipkin's political activism was quieter than Grossman's: he rarely fought for the right to publish a contentious work, and his and Lisnyanskaya's protests were expressed passively, for example by resignation from the Writers' Union. But he was troubled by the same official lie that tormented Grossman, Solzhenitsyn and other more or less dissident post-Stalinist writers: the Soviet authorities refused to recognize the Holocaust, portraying the death of millions of Soviet Jews as merely part of the martyrdom of the USSR, refusing to admit that the Gestapo and the NKVD, the Nazi and the Communist Parties were mirror images of each other, and limiting de-Stalinization to a slow programme of mean-minded 'rehabilitation' of some of Stalin's victims. Lipkin's poetry, not gathered in book form until the 1990s, is important as political testimony. Like his friend Grossman he dared to make the Holocaust his subject, and, like very few Russian poets, he mourned the premature deaths of those who returned, physically destroyed, from the GULAG.

Lipkin, like Grossman, wrote novels about Stalin's oppression. One of them, *Dekada*, is a thinly fictionalised account of Stalin's deportation in 1944 of the Balkar people from the North Caucasus, but their narrative and characterisation are wooden. Only when he has the challenge of a metrical framework, as in 'The Technical Lieutenant-Quartermaster', can Lipkin release his full creative powers to deal with the conflicts and the chaos of world war. Other Lipkin poems also have the force of a politically motivated novel: his long 'Nestor and Saria', about the murder of Nestor Lakoba, the charismatic and humane leader of Soviet Abkhazia in the 1920s and early 1930s, by Lavrenti Beria on Stalin's orders, is of great interest because of undocumented information that Lipkin obtained, as well as because of its pathos, for the Lakoba marriage was a tragic version of Lipkin's and Lisnyanskaya's happy union. The poem may have limited aesthetic merit, but it completes the picture of Lipkin's civic courage.

Much longer and more productive than that of the Brownings, the marriage of Lipkin and Lisnyanskaya is almost unique in the history of literature. Lisnyanskaya's poetry stretches over forty years and, like Lipkin's, relies very much on the classical Russian tradition. Both poets incorporate into the metaphysical tradition of nineteenth-century Russian poetry, of Tiutchev and Baratynski, Jewish elements of *kaddish* and Old Testament legends. Lisnyanskaya often sounds (and her poetry was particularly effective when read aloud) as if she had reincarnated Anna Akhmatova, by re-enacting the feelings of the Biblical Ruth, Shulamith or Lot's wife. The role of the wife mourning the destruction of the city and the family became only too apt for Soviet women poets. The interaction of Lipkin and Lisnyanskaya in their defence of oppressed writers and in their exchange of lyrical poems is a subject for future investigation, and it will be much helped by Yvonne Green's pioneering work of selection and translation.

Donald Rayfield
London

1

ANNA ANDREYEVNA
AKHMATOVA

These are my scattered memories of conversations with Anna Andreyevna Akhmatova: writers remember her room as cozy. It was in a pre-revolutionary building where the Ardovs lived in the legendary Ordynka.[1] Having originally been a maid's room, it was very small, with a high window almost right below the ceiling. Akhmatova became hard of hearing in her old age, but I found it difficult to speak to her loudly because everything we said could be heard next door in the main room where the family gathered. There were often noisy and cheerful visitors, old and young, writers and actors. Among the writers who often visited the house's owner was one who enjoyed particular notoriety and about whom Akhmatova had warned me. She discussed willingly, with me at least, burning political issues of the day but I didn't like to raise my voice in case a dangerous guest heard me. Was this legendary room really that cosy?

I'd met Akhmatova at Maria Petrovykh's[2] on Begovaya Street, at Nika Glen's[3] on Sadovaya-Karetnaya, at Bolshintsova-Stenich's on Korolenko Street in Sokolniki, (a fifth-floor flat in a building with no elevator), and at the home of Nina Leontyevna Manukhina (the poet Georgy Shengeli's[4] widow) on First Meschanskaya (now Mir). She was lovingly treated by her enthusiastic and respectful hosts in each of these places where she temporarily sheltered.

And yet she always yearned for Ordynka, even when she

---

1   +Bolshaya Ordynka is one of the oldest streets in central Moscow.
2   +Maria Sergeyevna Petrovykh (1908-1979), Russian poet and translator.
3   +Nika Nikolaevna Glen (1928-2005), translator.
4   +Georgy Shengeli (1894-1956), poet critic and translator.

was in the huge Manukhina-Shengeli apartment, where three women – mother, daughter, and their housekeeper – courted her, and she had at her disposal a large bright room and the late Shengeli's great library full of books written in different languages. Why, then, did Akhmatova yearn for the small room with a high window, almost right below the ceiling?

I think she was attracted not only by the kindness and self-less compassion of Nina Antonovna Olshevskaya[1], Ardov's[2] wife, an actress and theatre director, but also by the whole atmosphere of the Ardov's bustling actor family, the sweet boys Mike and Boris, the young visitors, the dinners, and midnight conversations at the wide table which was always set without a tablecloth. It seemed a bit like the Stray Dog to me.[3] But at the Stray Dog, everyone had been unhappy, a fact her poems attest to. But in Ordynka new voices, street jargon which hadn't yet become cliché could permeate her meager and tragically hard life. We had long conversations there, against the polyphony behind her wall.

I particularly remember something which other memoirs, however excellent, don't mention, not even the remarkable notes made by the author Lydia Chukovskaya.[4] Everyone knew that Nikolay Gumilyov[5] was shot because it was alleged he took part in Tagantsev's pro-monarchist conspiracy. Akhmatova had somehow gotten a copy of the young poet Irina Odoyevtseva's memoir *On the Banks of the Neva River*. In it, the author asserted that she [a friend of Gumilyov] had accidentally come across a stack of banknotes and a revolver in Gumilyov's

1   +Nina Antonovna Olshevskaya (1907-1991), actress.
2   +Viktor Efimovich Ardov (1900-1976), Russian writer.
3   +The Stray Dog Café in St Petersburg became famous in the early years of the 20th century thanks to the writers who often met there. These included the Acmeists; Nikolay Gumilyov, Osip Mandelstam and Mikhail Kuzmin. The name Stray Dog, appealed to their sense of isolation in aristocratic Russia.
4   +Lydia Korneyevna Chukovskaya (1907- 1996), Soviet writer and poet.
5   +Nikolay Stepanovich Gumilyov (1886-1921), poet and literary critic, Akhmatova's first husband.

drawer, which had led her to believe he'd participated in the conspiracy. Odoyevtseva painted Gumilyov as a heroic monarchist, a Russian André Chénier[1]. It was clear how displeased Akhmatova was when she read this beautiful fiction about the actions of the father, whose undeserved punishment had also included their son's imprisonment. Odoyevtseva's name was always linked dangerously to Akhmatova's after *On the Banks of the Neva River*. Akhmatova told me that she knew for certain that Gumilyov hadn't been a party to the so-called 'Tagantsev conspiracy.' That (and I'm quoting her), there'd been no such conspiracy: Petrograd's Cheka had invented it to improve their profile with their leaders in Moscow. She said that Gumilyov had been on his way to talk to what he called "Russia's first Russian Authorities," assuring her in these terms. "You'll see, they'll be Russia's first Russian Authorities."

She told me he loved working at Gorky's 'World Literature.'[2] And now, as I write these notes, it's been proved conclusively, as Akhmatova told me thirty years ago, that when Gumilyov was shot, he was innocent.[3]

Akhmatova also told me that during the war, Gumilyov became disenchanted with the royal dynasty, that Grishka Rasputin[4] disgusted him. She heard him say this when he returned from the front after a brief period. I once said to her that Gumilyov's talent most brightly expressed itself in *The Pillar of Fire*. Akhmatova agreed, saying "It was his last book.

---

1   +André Marie Chénier (1762-1794), French poet guillotined aged 31 for expressing monarchist sympathies.
2   +The World Literature Publishing House (Vsemirnaya Literatura) was established by Maxim Gorky (Alexei Maximovich Peshkov) in 1921 with the purpose of providing 'culture for the people.' It commissioned the translation of over 200 European classics.
3   +In 1922 the case against Gumilyov was declared a complete fabrication.
4   +Grigori Yefimovich Rasputin (1869-1916), was a Russian peasant, mystic, faith healer and private adviser to the Romanovs. He became an influential figure in Saint Petersburg after August 1915 when Tsar Nicolas II took command of the army at the front.

He had just started to develop as a poet. His thoughts had deepened, risen above domestic ritual Christianity, attained the highest Christian philosophy. No one knows how his life would have developed in subsequent years if he hadn't been shot, but it's undeniable that we would have had another great Russian poet."

When Gumilyov was arrested, Akhmatova went to ask Maxim Gorky to intercede. She told me Gorky behaved impeccably and rang both Lenin and Trotsky in her presence, but neither of their secretaries would put him through. He only reached Lunacharsky[1], who promised to talk to Lenin. But whether a conversation of that sort ever took place, she didn't know.

She also told me funnier stories about Gumilyov, which I'll pass on here in my own words. Gumilyov lectured aspiring poets in a literary studio. Gorky, Gumilyov's boss, once visited his class and when the audience dispersed, Gorky asked Gumilyov, "Tell me, does a poet need to know all this? Is it necessary?"

"It is necessary," Gumilyov said firmly. Then Gorky asked a tricky question: "Nikolai Stepanovich, what would you say about my poems?"

"I don't know. Frankly, I don't remember if I've read them."

Gorky was not offended, but he said, "But one of my poems was very well received, especially among the young, students and workers; it's still recited to this day. It's called 'The Stormy Petrel.'"

"Yes, yes, I do remember; a trochaic tetrameter with entirely female endings. The meter imitates Hiawatha's. Excuse me, Alexei Maximovich, but it's hopeless. One of your lines happened to catch my eye: 'Vysóko v gory vpolz uzh i leg tam' [The snake crawled high up the mountain and lay there]. If you understood Russian versification, you'd never make an

---

1   +Anatoly Lunacharsky (1875–1933), playwright, critic, journalist and the Soviet Union's first People's Commissar for Education.

amphibrachic foot out of monosyllabic words; it's not done, it's not literary. 'Vpolz uzh i leg tam.' Can't your well-tuned writer's ear hear that this juxtaposition's completely impossible, whether in poetry or prose?"

When Gumilyov told Akhmatova what had happened, she laughed but was also alarmed, in case Gorky had taken offense, would sack Gumilyov and leave him without the state rations that came with his job, without which survival in that year of famine would have been hard. But Gorky did not get angry. Moreover, he became, in Akhmatova's words, yet more respectful of Gumilyov.

Many things happened in that Ordynka room, even I can't remember them all. But every now and then, something re-emerges in my weakening recollection. Once I got home late at night after yet another translation meeting. Suddenly Akhmatova called me and said, "Come to me. Now."

"Shall we put it off until tomorrow? It's late ..." I said.

"I need you now ..." she said and hung up.

I got dressed, went down into the subway (fortunately, it was a direct line), and in forty minutes I was with her. It was obvious that she was very excited. She didn't recline on her firm couch as she usually did but walked around the room holding her hands up, which was unusual for her; her wrists were exposed. I thought something terrible had happened; Akhmatova had always had accurate premonitions.

"Read," she said and gave me a Russian magazine published abroad. I remember neither its name nor the author of the article that so excited Akhmatova. I vaguely imagined that it was Princess Shahovskaya. If I'm wrong, then I apologize to the reader forthwith.

I read the lines Akhmatova had indicated to me. They plunged me into bewilderment. I read them again and asked myself why she was reacting so emotionally. The article said (to the best of my recollection) that Gumilyov had abandoned the great poet Anna Akhmatova for the pretty, frivolous Anna

Engelhardt[1]. What was I supposed to say? What was so irritating? But Akhmatova had called me to come so late at night for a reason, so I said, "It's wrong to meddle in the personal life of a poet who, thank God, is still alive."

"Nonsense! What does personal life have to do with it?" Her voice rang with the anger her friends knew well. "Nikolay Stepanovich didn't abandon me; it was I who abandoned him!"

I was relieved; nothing serious had happened, and her anger touched and delighted me. The great, revered poet was still very much a woman. But to analyze that evening: all her life Akhmatova was exposed to the slander of her enemies, disloyal friends, petty individuals, and ferocious regimes. One of her poems is called 'Slander.' Her literary works were true, as were her all-too-brief memoirs. Her poems had magical, breathtaking precision; she hated inaccuracy in any genre and hated lies more. That trifle published in a foreign magazine was the last drop in the overflowing cup of her bitter life.

Like all of us, Akhmatova was outraged by the scandal that Khrushchev perpetrated in Manezh[2] when he attacked young artists. When we talked about it I remembered, for some reason, the phrase in Tamerlane's autobiography "The world is like a golden treasure chest filled with snakes and scorpions."

Akhmatova liked the phrase, but she talked of something else: "My Akhmatova ancestors were relatives to Princess Yusupov, and the Yusupovs descended from Tamerlane, who himself was a descendant of Genghis Khan; therefore, Genghis Khan is my ancestor."

I explained that this wasn't correct. The next day I brought her Timur's autobiography, translated by V Panov[3] from the

---

1   + Anna Engelhardt, Nikolay Gumilyov's second wife.
2   +In 1962, while visiting the "30 Years of the Moscow Artists' Union" art exhibition at Manezh Square, the then First Secretary of the Communist Party of the Soviet Union, Nikita Khrushchev, attacked its organisers for "filth, decadence and sexual deviations."
3   +Vasily Nikolayevich Panov (1906-1973), Soviet chess player and writer.

Turkic and Chaghatay. In his foreword and commentary, he denied Timur's claim that he was Genghis' grandson and said, "Autobiographical 'genealogy' usually links the 'hero' with a great ancestor." Akhmatova was clearly unhappy but came to terms with the fact that she was not descended from Genghis Khan, saying, "Being Tamerlane's descendant is still something." Since I was editing an edition of the classical Tatar poet, Ğabdulla Tukay, I suggested that Akhmatova translate something of his for the volume. She said, "Look. I am furious, but once that passes, of course I'll translate my fellow Tatar."[1]

One thing I came to understand about Akhmatova that I didn't notice when we first met was that, although her unique caliber was reflected in the level of her conduct and discourse, she never affected airs. She loved a joke, often made them herself, debunked those she esteemed without being judgmental, wore her Acmeism on her sleeve, understood Symbolism's importance as a phenomenon of Russia's public life but was sensitive to the long-standing antagonism of its elders, and found them, (with the exception of Blok[2]), to be personally flawed. I often listened keenly to her descriptions of Bryusov[3], Vyacheslav Ivanov[4], Balmont[5], Merezhkovsky[6], and

---

1   +The surname 'Akhmatova' is distinctly Tatar. Gorenko adopted it because her father did not want his name associated with poetry.

2   +Alexander Alexandrovich Blok (1880-1921), Russian poet.

3   +Valery Yakovlevich Bryusov (1873-1924), Russian poet and historian. He was one of the principal members of the Russian Symbolist movement.

4   +Vyacheslav Ivanov, (1866-1949), poet and playwrite. He was associated with the Russian Symbolist movement.

5   +Konstantin Dmitriyevich Balmont (1867-1942), Russian Symbolist poet, translator, one of the major figures of the Silver Age of Russian Poetry. He was associated with the Russian Symbolist movement.

6   +Dmitry Sergeyevich Merezhkovsky (1866-1941), novelist and literary critic. Together with Nikolai Minsky, he is regarded as the founder of Russian Symbolism.

Gippius[1]. She didn't like them.

She took a great interest in new Russian poetry and the huge crowds it attracted to readings. In my presence, she only praised Joseph Brodsky[2], whose stature as a poet she recognized early. Of another poet, older than Brodsky and widely published, she said, "elegant, but shallow." She would refute acclaimed talent: I remember commending someone reasonable, who was often sharply satirical. Her retort was, surprised: "Why would I need satire in verse?"

When Akhmatova came from Leningrad to Moscow, friends and acquaintances visited her daily. She didn't like it if several arrived at once: each was given not only a fixed day, but also an appointed time to call. I had my own slot and, once, when I arrived in Ordynka, I saw Boris Pasternak[3]. His appearance and behavior made it evident that he was about to leave but couldn't stop talking. For some reason, he spoke about Galsworthy, called *The Forsyte Saga* boring, strung out, lifeless. Soon after he left, Akhmatova cheered up.

"Can you guess why Borisik has suddenly pounced on Galsworthy? No? Once, many years ago, the English students nominated Pasternak for a Nobel Prize, but it was Galsworthy who got it."

"Anna Andreyevna," I said, "for goodness sake, is that worthy of you, such a great poet?"

"This great poet is a complete child!"

I should mention that this conversation took place long before Pasternak was awarded the Nobel Prize, that Akhmatova said "Borisik" very softly. She admired Pasternak's genius and firmly believed in the immortality of his poetry while sincerely doubting that of her own. She'd been happy, though somewhat

---

1   +Zinaida Nikolaevna Gippius (1869–1945), Russian poet, playwright, editor, short story writer and religious thinker.s She was a founding member of the Russian Symbolist movement.
2   +Joseph Aleksandrovich Brodsky (1940–1996), Russian poet and essayist.
3   +Boris Leonidovich Pasternak (1890–1960), Russian poet and novelist.

surprised when I'd told her she was the only successor to Nekrasov, that Nekrasov's plaintive, heart-rending anapest was heard in her lines from 'Requiem': "I nenuzhnym priveskom boltalsya / Vozle tyurem svoikh Leningrad" [Leningrad slumped around its prisons / Like a defeated emblem's remnants].

However, despite her doubts, as is often the case with great artists, Akhmatova guessed at her power and her place among the greats.

In 1958 or 1959, she phoned me and said that she was nearby at a friend's and wanted to come and see me. I later found out where she'd been. It was only a ten-minute walk away, but for her, that was by then too demanding, so she took a taxi.

I put a bottle of "Lydia" on the table, the Moldovan wine which was in fashion then, but Akhmatova said she didn't like it.

"Some vodka?" I suggested.

"A little bit, with pleasure, although it's against doctor's orders," Akhmatova said, taking out some pills from her pocket, either nitroglycerin or Validol. I was healthy then and didn't know what these drugs were for. We drank a glass of liqueur each, then another, and then I drank alone while Akhmatova read me a chapter from 'Poem Without a Hero.' It was so new, powerful, unlike what she'd done before, yet so Akhmatova. Alive, clever, it shone. I was shocked, told Anna Andreyevna that none of Russia's poets understood with such depth her pain and her life. None had described the first decade after the 20th century, before the war, how different our lives could have been had it not been for the First World War, its effect on the Tsarist government, and the terrible demands it made on her people. I said that she, Akhmatova, was the first to do so, and she blushed, either from the alcohol or from what I'd said. She praised me, saying, "No one understands verse like you do."

She was usually only warm in that way to the Chukovskys

(father and daughter), but that night she became playful and a joyful atmosphere ensued. I drank half a bottle of vodka, forgot my usual trepidation, and said, "So, who is there? Among women, Akhmatova is above all. Well, who preceded her, who follows? Leaving aside Tsvetaeva: I like her lyrical poems and several poems from the books which followed them, but I don't like her long poems, except for 'The Rat Catcher' and 'The Mountain's Poem.' Akhmatova smiled, said nothing, and I let my ideas run on: "In the 18th century, there was a poetess called Bunin, related to Ivan[1]."

"Nobody read her. I didn't. Next!"

"Evdokia Rostopchina.[2]"

"Very superficial."

"Karolina Pavlova.[3]"

"Valuable, but not first class."

"Mirra Lokhvitskaya.[4]"

"Something sang in her. But her poetry bears the stamp of the era's stagnation as did Nadson's[5], Minsky's[6], Fofanov's.[7]"

"Who then is left? Only Sappho?[8]"

"Sappho is a lovely myth. Vyacheslav Ivanov read it to me in Greek. From Sappho's lines, only ruins remained."

"Of course, I didn't read Sappho in the original, only Vyacheslav Ivanov's translations in his *Alcaeus and Sappho*. I'll name the last one, Desbordes-Valmore[9]. Pasternak compared

---

1   +Ivan Alekseyevich Bunin (1870-1953), the first Russian writer to win the Nobel Prize for Literature.

2   +Evdokia Petrovna Rostopchina (1811-1858), Russian poet.

3   +Karolina Karlovna Pavlova (1807-1893), Russian poet and novelist.

4   +Mirra Lokhvitskaya (1869-1905), Russian poet.

5   +Semyon Yakovlevich Nadson (1862-1887), Russian poet.

6   +Nikolai Maksimovich Minsky (1855-1937), poet of the 'Silver Age.'

7   +Konstantin Mikhailovich Fofanov (1862-1911), Russian poet.

8   +Ancient Greek poet.

9   +Marceline Desbordes-Valmore (1786-1859), French poet and novelist.

Tsvetaeva with her."[1]

"Even Pushkin wrote about the weakness of French poetry. After all, there had been neither Baudelaire[2] nor Verlaine[3] yet. Desbordes-Valmore was nice but too sentimental and naive," Akhmatova replied with vehemence.

A few years after this spontaneous conversation, an important event happened in my life: important because it was associated with Akhmatova. I had a poetry reading scheduled by the VTO.[4] It was the first time my own poems were read publically. Anna Andreyevna became excited: "I want to come." I asked, even begged Akhmatova not to. It would be demanding for her; the hall might be stuffy, the elevator, as was often the case, might be out of order. Nina Antonovna Olshevskaya[5] was reading with me, but Akhmatova kept stubbornly repeating, "I want to come. I have to."

And she did. To this day, the organizers of the readings at the VTO recall proudly that Akhmatova came; they even add that Akhmatova approved of their events, but the truth was that Anna Andreyevna attended only to help her obscure, middle-aged friend.

In 1961 I finished my epic poem 'The Technical Lieutenant-Quartermaster.'[6] Anna Andreyevna said she wanted to listen to it. She then lived on Prospekt Mia at Nina Leontyevna Manukhina-Shengeli's[7] house, where I visited frequently (I'd

---

1   +Olga Peters Hasty, *Tsevateva's Orphic Journey's in the Worlds of the Word*,(Northwestern University Press, 1966), p137. fn. 4.
2   +Charles Pierre Baudelaire (1821–1867), French poet.
3   +Paul-Marie Verlaine (1844–1896), French poet associated with the Symbolist movement.
4   +VTO (Vserossiyskoye Teatral'noye Obshchestvo), the principal actors and theatrical workers' union of Russia founded in 1887.
5   +Nina Antonovna Olshevskaya (1907–1991), actress.
6   +Semyon Izrailevich Lipkin's epic poem, translated by Yvonne Green and Sergei Makarov in *A Close Reading of 53 Poems by Semyon Izrailevich Lipkin* (Hendon Press, 2023).
7   +Georgy Shengelli's widow.

been a friend of the late Arbatov and was a member of the commission on his literary heritage, which used to meet there).

I read the long poem to both Anna Andreyevna and Nina Leontyevna. It took more than an hour. I saw tears in Anna Andreyevna's eyes. The summer that followed, Anna Andreyevna gave me a little booklet published by the Library of Soviet Poetry. This is how it was inscribed on the back cover:

To Lipkin, whose poems I always hear and once wept. Akhmatova, July 6 1961.[1]

I have several of Akhmatova's books with kind inscriptions, but this one is my most treasured. It wasn't only a source of pride but also buttressed my sense of a right to exist when it was denied to me during the nineteen eighties by my homeland and its press.

---

1   +Stikhotoreniya 1909-1960 (Poems 1909-1960).

2

AN EVENING AND A DAY WITH MARINA TSVETAEVA

At the end of November or in early December 1940, I received a telephone call from my friend, the poet and translator Vera Zvyaginsteva[1]: "Marina Tsvetaeva[2] would like to meet you. Come round tonight."

Responding to the amazement in my voice, she added, "I can't make head or tail of it. She is, of course, totally unaware of your poetry."

I was overcome because I had known Tsvetaeva's name since my early youth when I'd bought her book *Versty*[3] at a giveaway price from a market stall in Odesa. The freshness and vehemence of those poems swept me off my feet, and within a few days, I knew the entire book by heart.

I'd heard that Tsvetaeva had returned from Paris, where she had become a celebrated poet, and that her daughter and husband had returned before her. Moscow's old literary circles were all talking about Marina as though she were an empress; they never used her surname. Her daughter and husband's horrible fates were as yet unknown to me.

On the appointed day and hour, I visited Zviaginsteva's home, and Marina Ivanovna was there. My first impression was of a woman advanced in age, with graying hair, a rugged grey face and distinctive eyes which protruded and were very expressive. It wasn't clear if she noticed me as we spoke. Her movements were fast and abrupt; she tossed her head like a young woman and wore a dark, loose-fitting dress which was

---

1   +Vera Klavdievna Zvyagintseva (1894-1972), Russian actress, poet, translator and memoirist.
2   +Marina Ivanovna Tsvetaeva (1912-1941), Russian poet.
3   +Measure of distance in pre-revolutionary Russia.

almost like a nun's habit and very unconventional.

After the social niceties and some wine, Marina Ivanovna expressed a wish to read her poem 'Attempt at a Room.' She explained that the poem was an answer to a question once asked by Rilke about the room where they would meet. They never, in fact, met but corresponded. She recited from memory; her voice was fresh, charming, simple and cadenced, her accent Muscovite. When she finished, there was an awkward silence for a while.

I didn't immediately like the poem. Many years later, I reread it and found some profound thought and heard its music, but my opinion remained unchanged. My friends didn't like it either, and if contemporary readers brand us old fashioned and narrow minded, I would have trouble arguing the case. I don't remember what we talked about after she read.

About midnight we left, and I took Marina Ivanovna home: she lived nearby then. She explained that she'd been asked to edit a French translation of the Kalmyk national epic *Dzhangar*, done by a Frenchman living in Moscow, from my Russian version.[1] She asked numerous questions about its rhyme scheme and form and touched on Kalmyk culture and terminology. After a long discussion about the epic itself, she said: "I don't really like your method of translation. Some of the stories you've told me are lovely, but they're better than your translations."

And when we were at her front door, she asked whether I liked walking, and when I said I did, she offered to meet me the next day for a walk round Moscow. We arranged to meet by a metro station. I suggested picking her up by taxi, and she said, "I am not used to taxis."

The next day she appeared at our meeting place promptly. She wore a blue beret and an ankle-length trench coat, which looked unseasonably light to me. It was already cold, and there

---

1   +Kalmyk Book Publishers 1971 repr. 1977.

was a sparse covering of snow on the ground. On Marina Ivanovna's initiative, we walked across Red Square towards Zamoskvorechye.[1] She knew the area well and told me its old street names, pointing out houses where its famous writers and playwrights used to live. She was the first person I'd met who'd been abroad, and I asked insatiably about [other expatriate writers] Bunin, Khodasevich[2], Adamovich[3], Balmont, Gippius, Nabokov[4], and Merezhkovsky. We discussed contemporary Soviet poets and the way they were perceived by Russian émigrés. For example, she said Adamovich and Nabokov recognize only Akhmatova and Mandelstam[5], that they didn't accept the great Pasternak, couldn't stand Mayakovsky[6], and that the young loved Bagritsky[7].

We discussed her poem, 'You Throw Back Your Head Because You're An Arrogant Liar' which, I did not know at the time, was dedicated to Mandelstam. To start with, she rejected my preference for the original line, "We are like two solemn foreigners" over the later version, "We are jingling karbovanets[8]" saying, "Your ideas about poetry are antediluvian."

I explained that, metrically, she'd accented "Karbovanets" on the wrong syllable. She listened and promised to consider what I'd said.

After we'd walked for hours in Zamoskvorechye, she told me

---

1 +A district of Moscow relatively close to the Kremlin but on the opposite bank of the river.

2 +Vladislav Felitsianovich Khodasevich (1886-1939), Russian poet and literary critic who presided over the Berlin circle of Russian emigre litterateurs.

3 +Georgy Viktorovich Adamovich (1892-1972, Russian poet of the Acmeist school, literary critic, translator and memoirist).

4 +Vladimir Vladimirovich Nabokov, Russian (1899-1977), American novelist.

5 +Osip Emilyevich Mandelstam (1891-1938), Russian poet and essayist.

6 +Vladimir Mayakovsky (1893-1930), poet, playwrite, screenwriter, Bolshevik politician leading futurist, painter, propagandist, founder of Left Front of Art (LEF).

7 +Eduard Georgiyevich Bagritsky (1895-1934), poet.

8 +Ukranian coin.

with simplicity worthy of Tolstoy or Rousseau that she needed a restroom. Away from Moscow's center, finding one remains a problem even today; before the war it was worse. I remembered that at Big Polianka, which we'd just passed, I had spotted an Executive Committee's sign, and I led Marina Ivanovna back there authoritatively. We walked into the building, I quickly found what my companion needed, and when we left, Tsvetaeva said, "Is it what all Muscovites do?"

I said, wanting to make her smile, "Only those who understand the value of Executive Committees." She didn't smile or even notice my joke and I saw her shrug her shoulders through her unseasonably thin foreign raincoat.

She told me about her friend Balmont, who was impoverished and had almost lost his memory, about the Merezhkovskys, answered me when I questioned her eagerly about Khodasevich. We talked also about Soviet poets. I remember she mentioned Kirsanov[1] and called his versification "A life-sized engine given to a toy truck."

We spent two hours at the museum her father had established.[2] Marina got hungry. I was looking forward to treating her to a sumptuous dinner at The National.[3] I had the money. But Marina, despite her myopia, noticed a canteen close to the museum on Gritsevets Street. It was cheap: the men building the metro went there. No matter how hard I tried to convince Marina Ivanovna, emphasizing the fact that it was just an ordinary café and that The National was nearby, she wouldn't listen to me. It was dimly lit and stuffy, we were overwhelmed by the cloying smell of the sauerkraut soup cooked there every day. We carried our trays of poorly washed dishes to the self-service line and then sat at a dirty table. But Marina devoured the soup, bread, meat cutlets, and over-cooked sticky pasta with relish. She took out of her pocket a piece of paper with a few

---

1   +Semyon Kirsanov (1906-1972), Ukranian poet of Jewish origin.
2   +The Pushkin Museum of Fine Arts.
3   +An hotel opened in 1903.

printed lines on it and gave it to me saying, "A review on my collection for *The Soviet Writer* by Zelinsky."[1] I recently learned that what she'd shown me was only the end of that review. It had been so vile in its entirety that the publisher had decided only to send Marina Ivanovna a part of it (at that time, reviews were usually shown to authors). Tsvetaeva's piece of paper said that the reviewer didn't see anything politically harmful in her poems but said our Soviet poetry had advanced so far that her poetic experiments would seem to the reader to belong to a long-superseded genre, to be anachronistic. This was given as a reason not to publish her collection.

We parted late that night and never met again, although we spoke on the phone a few times.

---

1   +Kornely Zelinsky (1896-1970), an official literary critic.

3

THE FATE OF VASILY GROSSMAN

I found this docket in my papers:

> We, the undersigned, warrant that Comrade Lt Col
> V S Grossman, The Red Star newspaper's Special War
> Correspondent, has worn out his great coat after three
> years' work at the front.

>   Colonel (I Khitrov)
>   Colonel (P Kolomiytsev)
>   Lieutenant Colonel (L Gatovsky)
>   July 28, 1944

Every phrase is accurate: "three years of work at the front"
means work performed in the smoke and fire of attack, in the
mud and snow of impassable roads, in dusty trenches, in the
blood of the wounded, in swamp, river, and lake water. When
I was in Stalingrad, I saw famous writers, who served as war
correspondents for central newspapers, go out for a day with
the troops, but their courage was somehow always short-lived.
They spent most of their time drinking in the officers' dugouts.
Their courage, as Lermontov observed of Grushnitsky's,
"wasn't very Russian."[1] Grossman's, by contrast, made him a
foot soldier of war's brutal poetry. While other correspondents
had their uniforms fitted by tailors, once and sometimes even
twice a year, Grossman's overcoat was worn out, mud soiled,
petrol stained. That's how I remember him in Stalingrad.

For my part, I always seemed to be in the wrong place at
the wrong time. I survived the War but was otherwise jinxed.
My first posting was on the Baltic as a correspondent with the
marines, and I do not need to narrate here what conditions

---

1   +Mikhail Lermontov, *A Hero of Our Time* (Penguin Classics, 2009).

were like during the Siege of Leningrad. After several months, I found myself seconded to the non-Russian forces of the 110th Kalmyk Cavalry Division. We were encircled at Mechetinskaya in July 1942. Our squad became detached and roamed the steppe behind German lines until we emerged near Mozdok in August. After that, I was sent to join Stalingrad's flotilla on the Volga. I was on the gunboat Usyskin when it sank, leaving us to cross to the German-occupied right bank in armored motorboats and make for Colonel Gorokhov's 'Marketplace' stronghold and Colonel Rodimtsev's 'Drainpipe' headquarters. Neither personal courage nor fighting spirit drove me. I just followed orders.

While the frozen Volga was being bombarded, Commissar Usyskin asked me one day if I'd like to cross it. He and two of his crew were delivering letters, vodka, and other special supplies to some of our marines who'd set up an observation post in the attic of a burnt-out building in the middle of German-occupied Stalingrad. I only went with them because I couldn't face my cowardice.

Grossman was different. Moscow's readers, not Stalin's Commanders, drove his actions. No one at the front gave him orders. He searched out the truth with the focus and bravery of a real artist, pursued it in the line of fire as death howled and sang over his head. God kept him; no German bullet ever wounded him, but in later times others of his own would do so.

Grossman was principled in war and despised writers who kowtowed to authority, courted honors, demanded preferment and promotions or were too lazy to go to the front. He was a faithful husband, unlike many of us sinners.

His palpable moral stature intimidated some people. When we went into Germany, and the shameful orgy of the victors began, one of the front lines' most famous poets parodied a popular song:

> While we rape and burn
> Vasily Grossman looks and thinks

Will man ever learn?[1]

A ditty went round about a *Pravda* journalist sending loot to his relative Samuil Samosud, the Bolshoi conductor:

Your family do well out of your job,
If only you wrote as well as you rob,
But the Maestro's happy at any rate,
Eating off German silver and plate.

I'm going to discuss *For A Just Cause* and *Life and Fate*, Grossman's Stalin duologue, not only because they mark the last years of his life but because they constitute literary and national emblems. Their immeasurable destiny drove one of the 20th century's greatest Russian writers to an early grave. As his only surviving friend, his closest for over twenty years, I feel I have to draw something of a portrait of him, even if there are things I still can't say.

We were kindred spirits, daily companions, but his skill and sensitivity far exceeded mine. I once heard Andrei Platonov[2] call him 'The Christ', and I understood why.

I'll try and sketch Grossman's literary and personal history as I saw it, for now, and hope to be spared having to improve on this account over time.

We met shortly before the War. Semyon Gecht, who, like me, came from Odesa, introduced us. Although Grossman's literary career was just starting, he was already respected in literary circles and his reputation exceeded that of his well-known namesake L P Grossman, a critic and the author of *The Notes of D'Arshiak,* a popular novel about Pushkin's duel. Vasily Grossman's first short story 'In the Town of Berdichev' had already been published to critical acclaim in the Soviet writers' official journal, *Literaturnaya Gazeta*, in April 1934. Our best writers recognized the artist's original talent immediately.

---

1   +It is estimated that two million German women were raped by Soviet soldiers.
2   +Andrei Platonov (1899–1951), Soviet author and fierce critic of Stalinism.

Babel[1] told me that Odesa, the Ukraine's Jewish capital city, had been seen with new eyes, and Bulgakov[2] commented on how incredible it was that something so worthwhile could still be published.

Later, I read Grossman's first novel *Gluckauf.* Its German title can be translated as *Elated to be Elevated* and alluded to the way our deep-seam miners met their comrades when they surfaced after a shift. After Grossman had studied Chemistry at Moscow University, he'd worked as an analyst at the Smolyanka-2 coal mines, which he'd proudly tell people were the deepest and hottest shafts in the country.

For me, *Glaukauf* vivifies the hard and dangerous challenges met by Donbas' miners, face workers, lumbermen, and horse drivers. But it was a manuscript which enraged Gorky to whom Grossman had it sent through a relative of his who was, at that time, well placed in The Party.

Gorky's report on *Glaukauf* included the following: "[Grossman] describes things the way he sees them, which is one approach. But to get something across, you have to ask yourself the question, why do I write, what truths am I trying to convey?"

Isn't it strange that Gorky, who had such talent– and truth is always at the root of an artist's talent – could at that time assert that truth was relative? It should be noted that this was a man who, after Lenin condemned him, would turn to God in a search for the ultimate truth.

When Gecht introduced me to Grossman, the War had already started in the West, but Moscow was peaceful and bright. Grossman, his wife Olga Mikhailovna, Gecht, and I made our way to a table at the summer ice cream parlor on

---

1   +Isaac Babel (1894-1940), writer, journalist, playwright, and literary translator. Executed by the NKVD in 1940.

2   +Mikhail Bulgakov (1891-1940), Russian writer and author of *The Master and Margarita.*

Tverskoy Boulevard. I'd just read *Stepan Kol'chugin*[1] and told Grossman I thought it was well written but that the image of the old Bolshevik, Bakhmutsky, seemed ill-conceived, that he looked more like a Menshevik, and if he kept writing him as he had done so far, the character was unlikely to work in the novel's second installment. Grossman's lips spread into a smile, he put his thumbs to his crooked fingertips and brought his hands up to his glasses like binoculars, something he'd do when someone had hit the nail on the head in a discussion. Grossman never finished *Stepan Kol'chugin*.

I recognized Grossman's wide-eyed, blond Malorossian wife from somewhere but couldn't place her. Grossman later told me Olga had been Boris Guber's wife. Guber was a descendant of the poet Edward Guber, Pushkin's contemporary, who translated *Faust*.

At this point, I'll digress to raise The Pereval Group, of which Boris Guber was a member and which Aleksandr Voronsky[2] headed. After the Civil War, Lenin told Voronsky to collect new Soviet literature. Although I never knew much about The Pereval Group's work, I can say that my literary friends and I thought they were engaged in a principled search for true, non-careerist Russian literature, unlike RAPP's gangsters[3], Auerbach[4] and later Safronov[5].

Bear in mind Pereval was working against a tide of anti-Russian criticism. Nikolai Zarudin[6] (like Boris Pil'nyak, a German who wrote Russian) found his work pilloried by critics

---

1   +A novel that Grossman published in installments between 1937 and 1940.
2   +Aleksandr Voronsky (1884-1937), literary critic and editor. known for his humanist take on Marxism.
3   +Russian Association of Proletarian Writers (RAPP), a literary association in the USSR post-revolutionary era (1928-1932).
4   +Leopold Auerbach (1903-1937), Soviet literary critic and editor, a Komsomol activist. Notorious for his aggressive pro-regime literary criticism.
5   +Anatoly Vladimirovič Safrornov (1911-1990), Head of the Writers' Union, an organ of officialdom.
6   +Nikolai Zarudin (1899-1937), writer and poet.

loyal to the RAPP. They said he'd be at home in Billingsgate Market, calling his wares, which were the demise of Russia's soul, which was a good thing too. Pereval was doomed. Pil'nyak was very close not just to Voronsky but to the rest of the organization's backbone, Ivan Kataev[1], Nikolai Zarudin, Abram Lezhnev[2], Pyotr Pavlenko[3], and Efim Vikhrev[4], who was the first person to write about Palekh[5].

It has been asserted that Pavlenko destroyed Pereval, but he was just a tool. I was closest to Lezhnev and Pil'nyak, but I knew the others. Now Moscow has thousands of writers, but then there was paucity, and we who were anthologized in thick journals knew one another, whether as newcomers or old masters.

When Pereval was disbanded, but its writers weren't yet repressed, I once happened on Voronsky on the narrow staircase of the Goslitizdat[6] in Bol'shoi Cherkassky Street, where he worked as a series editor. I asked him how he and Abram Lezhnev were.

Voronsky, a seminary scholar, said in ecclesiastical tones, "'Back to your tents, O Israel',[7] let's go home and start our own kingdom; we've no place in this one," and went into his office. I think this would have been a year before his arrest, when he was still young and strong, and his graying hair made him look distinguished.

Grossman, who came to Moscow from the Donbas after he and his first wife divorced, was befriended by Pereval,

---

1   +Ivan Kataev (1902-1937), Soviet novelist, short story writer, and journalist.
2   +Abram Lezhnev (1893-1938), Soviet writer who defended Shostakovitch in 1936 and was later shot in the purges.
3   +Pyotr Pavlenko (1899-1951), an establishment novelist who's work exemplifies social realism.
4   +Efim Fedorovich Vikhrev (1901-1935), writer and author of *The People of Palekh*.
5   +Palekh - Russian urban locality known for its iconography and art.
6   +Publishing house of Soviet Literature.
7   +The First Book of Kings, 12-16.

who welcomed him warmly. I think the character of Vavilova in his first story appealed to them. She was written without the partisan romanticism of those years as a pregnant Red Army Commissar who lived in a hut in Berdichev during the Civil War. This was what appealed to the Pereval authors. No one had written like that about "our young girls in military uniform"[1] before.

And through Pereval, Grossman fell in love with Olga Mikhailovna. In 1937 Boris Guber was arrested along with other Pereval members. Soon, Olga was taken too. Her two sons by Guber, Michael and Fyodor, stayed in Grossman's care. He told me, "You cannot imagine what life is like for a man in whose hands are small children and whose wife is arrested." Then he did something that only a man like Grossman could have done. He wrote a letter to Yezhov, the almighty 'Iron Commissar' of the NKVD[2], saying that Olga was his wife, not Guber's, and as such, she should not be subject to arrest. This might seem a simple ploy, but in 1937 only a very brave man would have dared to write a letter like that to the State's chief executioner. Fortunately and unexpectedly, the letter worked. After spending about a year in the women's prison (which was located in a lane behind the present-day American Embassy), Olga was released. (Incidentally, while she was in prison, Olga heard rumors that Maria Spiridonova[3] had been held there for a period.)

When I met Grossman, I felt his contentedness. He was enjoying literary success, especially significant after the meager, lonely life of an engineer at Donbas (his first wife and daughter Katya had lived separately in Kyiv); new intelligent and interesting friends, and a beautiful new wife. "It struck me: what beautiful wives writers have," he said to me when we became

---

1   +Popular song lyrics.

2   +NKVD – Soviet secret police (formerly named Cheka, later KGB).

3   +Maria Alexandrovna Spiridonova (1881-1941), leader of the left wing of the Socialist Revolutionary Party.

closer, and he recollected his early steps in the literary world. He was tall, curly-haired, and when he laughed – he laughed often in those days – his cheeks dimpled. His myopic eyes were unusual, inquisitive, questioning, searching, and kind, a rare combination. Women liked him. He emanated health. At that time, I still did not know that he was afraid to cross Moscow's squares and wide roads; he shared this agoraphobic trait with my other great friend, Anna Akhmatova.

Going back to our first meeting in the ice cream parlor, Gecht asked me to recite a few poems. Gecht and Olga listened indifferently, but Grossman said, "A baker," and went on to say that in the nineteenth century, poets were bakers, and in the twentieth, they became jewelers. Years on, he quoted this bakers and jewelers reference in his last book, *Dobro Vam*[1], which I'll talk about later.

Our first meeting was followed by others, sometimes at his communal apartment in Herzen Street opposite The Conservatory, sometimes at Gecht's or Fraerman's[2], where Paustovsky[3], Osip Cherny[4] and sometimes Gaidar[5] joined us. Grossman and I were drawn to each other, and then war interrupted our contact. On its fifth day, I was called up, and together with Alexander Kron and Leonid Solovyev (author of *Disturber of the Peace*[6]), I was sent to Kronstadt, while Grossman went to the front as a member of the staff of

---

1 +*Dobro Vam* was Grossman's original title for this work. It is the Russian translation of the formal Armenian greeting 'Barev dzez.' It has been published in English as *An Armenian Sketchbook*, trans. Robert Chandler (MacLehose Press, 2013).

2 +Ruvim Fraerman (1891-1972), a Russian children's writer.

3 +(1892-1968), Russian Soviet writer nominated for the Nobel Prize for literature in 1965.

4 +Edited *The Complete Black Book of Soviet Jewry*.

5 +(1904-1941), real name Golikov, both a famous writer and Red Army field commander known for his courage and ruthlessness.

6 +(1906-1962), a playwright and writer.

Krasnaya Zvezda [*The Red Star*]¹. We next saw each other in October 1942 in Stalingrad, where my Volga Flotilla was based, or rather, on the left bank of the Volga opposite Stalingrad. Our meeting wasn't coincidental. He knew that I was nearby, and our meeting would enable him to talk to the marines with whom I was stationed.

He was thin, unshaven, his coat was dirty and his searching eyes burned animatedly. We drank vodka in the cabin I shared with the engine room chief and then went down to the beach to talk heart-to-heart without interference. By then, I'd been on the Stalingrad front for just two weeks, whereas he had already gone through all the circles of hell throughout August and September and had been scorched by the Stalingrad fire, which he afterward described so powerfully in the novel, *For A Just Cause*. While we talked, I told him that we had a Ukrainian supply room midshipman called Shulz, who was always in demand. Seamen on the bank kept shouting, "Shulz! Shulz!" which scared an important political worker from Moscow, who thought the Germans had got to our shore. We had, I added, another seaman with an obviously German name, armored tanker commander First Sergeant Kautsky, but he was Jewish. Grossman smiled, then said reproachfully: "Jokes, jokes, while people are dying, and what wonderful people. Stalingrad is almost entirely in the hands of the Germans, but here will be the beginning of our victory. You agree with me?" I replied that in military affairs, I was poorly versed, but what I knew was that all would depend on God's will.

Grossman was convinced that the War was between Internationalism and Fascism. This war, in his opinion, would wash away all the Stalinist stain from Russia's faces, that the holy blood of this war would cleanse us of the blood of the innocent dispossessed, of the blood of 1937. I do not remember every word of his subsequent argument, but what he then said was essentially what he was later to write in *For A Just Cause*:

---

1 +The Soviet Army's daily newspaper.

The Party, its Central Committee, the political commissars of divisions and regiments, of companies and platoons, and the ordinary communists asserted in these battles the military and moral power of the Red Army.

I followed Grossman to Srednyaya Akhtuba, where he was collecting a car. All the long way there, we walked almost wordlessly, parted coldly, dissatisfied with one another.

We never met in Stalingrad again. I don't remember when he left, but he did not see our entry into the city. I told him later how, on the night of victory, February 3, I had walked on the Volga's ice with marines carrying bread, vodka, squeeze-boxes and multicolored rockets for the city residents.

Grossman's 'Stalingrad Sketches' made his name widely known both in the army and on the home front. They were regularly published in *The Red Star*, the most widely read newspaper during the war years. I believe some of them were published abroad. 'In the Line of the Main Drive' was especially famous. In it, one could literally hear the howl of air, reddened by bombs, the roar that "could stun mankind," in which there was a fire that "could burn and destroy a whole state." Stalin ordered *Pravda* to reprint the essay from *The Red Star*, although he did not like Grossman. We all knew that before the War, Stalin had personally crossed out *Stepan Kol'chugin* from the list of literary works previously unanimously approved by the Committee for the Stalin Prizes. Stalin called the novel 'Menshevik.' Unaware of Stalin's action, people from the country's major newspapers telephoned Grossman to congratulate him the night before the publication of the winners' list. A few years later, when Grossman told me about the incident, he said with a sly laugh, "You showed class feeling; your opinion coincided with Stalin's." 'In the Line of the Main Drive' fascinated the entire country. Its detail, the burning truth of battle, gave rise to the idea that "heroism had become a matter of everyday habit." "Now you can get everything you ask for," said Ehrenburg[1] to Grossman. But Grossman asked for nothing.

His fame grew with the publication of his novella, *The People Immortal*, his first relatively large literary work about the Great Patriotic War. Even after the publication abroad of the later novella, *Everything Flows*, and of *Life and Fate*, *The People Immortal* was lauded in our press, although less frequently. Despite the fact it was written eloquently, *The People Immortal* didn't move me.

In the summer of 1943, I was summoned to the Moscow Voenmorizdat[2] to discuss the publication of a book of my sketches about fighting from the gunboat Usyskin. I had to make changes and consider the usual editorial comments. I have to admit that I was glad to receive that invitation to go to Moscow. It turned out that Grossman and Platonov were in the capital. They'd come from the front for a meeting of military correspondents. I do not remember where we met; it could have been in the eighth room of The Writers' House where war reporters, summoned to Moscow for whatever reason, could get a tolerable and – for wartime – relatively copious lunch. Some of the diners you saw in the eighth room had never smelled powder; they were known as zemhusars.

Grossman and I embraced each other warmly, the cold Stalingrad meeting behind us. I did not recognize Platonov in his army captain's uniform: we'd previously had only a nodding acquaintance. As Platonov saw me, he muttered, with some irony: "A seaman, handsome in himself."[3] I think that Grossman befriended Platonov during the War since both served on *The Red Star*.

One day, Grossman told me, they'd had to go by car to the front on an empty winter road. Their driver was an elderly,

---

1 +Ilya Ehrenburg (1891–1967), Soviet writer. He edited *The Black Book* with Grossman. He was a journalist, translator, and cultural figure.
2 +The navy's publishing house.
3 +A line from a popular Russian song (author unknown).

short, ugly Tatar whose name was Seyfutdinov, but Platonov called him Sulfidinov. This 'Sulfidinov' enjoyed great success with women. Shivering and exhausted, they'd stopped at a hut not far from the front. The youngish hostess glanced at the driver. "Sulfidinov," said Platonov, "screw her and then ask her to fry eggs for us."

We agreed we'd meet in the evening at Platonov's. Since Platonov's family hadn't been evacuated, there'd be a homey atmosphere there. It was decided that we'd each try to bring some alcohol.

Unusually, Platonov lived with his family in their own apartment at Herzen Street, which had two adjacent rooms. They never starved but still had to count every penny. Suggestions that he was the building's janitor are unfounded.

Platonov had been persecuted from the very first day of his entry into the literary world. It was said that Stalin wrote a single word in the margin of Platonov's, *Vprok, For Future's Sake*, also known as *A Poor Man's Chronicles*[1]: 'scum.' After that, all hell broke loose for Platonov.

Fadeyev[2], the editor of *Red Virgin Soil*, the journal in which *For Future's Sake* was published, attacked Platonov in an article describing him as having launched an enemy-class onslaught. Fadeyev's minions (who were themselves subsequently and miserably pursued as "cosmopolitan"[3]) joined him in trampling Platonov underfoot. Among them I particularly remember Gurvich. The Old Testament God of vengeance punished Gurvich. As for Fadeyev, he was insincere – in this instance and in many others. In truth, he valued Platonov; his taste was

---

1 +Published in 1931 in the *Krasnaya nov'* (Red Virgin Soil [1921-1942]), literary journal.

2 +A A Fadeyev (1901-1956). The first head of RAPP, he became leader of The Writers' Union in 1934, and subsequently its secretary. He committed suicide after the Twentieth Party Congress.

3 +During the 1948-1951 campaign of an anti-semitic nature against 'routeless cosmopolitans' which were the terms Stalin adopted to denote Jews.

generally good and he had linguistic sensitivity, but he invariably, with a Bartholomew-like frenzy, followed Stalin's dictates to the letter.

Despite the terrible review by the editor, Platonov was not arrested, though everything he published was subjected to such destructive criticism that everyone thought he was doomed. He had a hard life, surviving from day to day. He wrote a play for children with Fraerman and adapted fairy tales. But his talent was so original that even works he wrote to earn his daily bread confounded editors and were rarely published or remunerated.

In those years, the literary environment was more important than it is now (I don't know if such an environment could be said to exist at all today). Its opinions were powerful enough to compete with those of the State, and there were writers who invoked Platonov's name with deep respect, often with admiration. An example was when *The Literary Critic Journal*[1] suddenly took a decision not to toe the establishment's line, published some of Platonov's short stories, and outraged both literary and non-literary mandarins. Platonov also wrote critiques which the journal, led by a political refugee, the Hungarian Marxist philosopher György Lukács[2], and another Marxist, Mikhail Lifshitz[3], decided to publish, giving Platonov the pen name of Chelovekov.[4] This alias may not have been accidental: Platonov used to say that he would like to write a novel called *Journey into Man's Depths*, a title parodying popular books like *Journey into the Depths of Africa*.

With rare exceptions, I personally did not like Platonov's critical work, but he did write a good article about Akhmatova.

---

1 +Published from 1933-1940.
2 +György Lukács (1885-1971), a Hungarian Marxist philosopher, aesthetician, literary historian, and critic. He was one of the founders of Western Marxism.
3 +Mikhail Lifshitz (1905-1983), a Soviet literary critic and philosopher of art. As an academic philosopher, Lifshitz served as an executive member of Soviet Academy of Sciences from 1975. In the early 1930s he was a close associate of György Lukács.
4 +From the Russian 'tchelovek', the man.

His literary views often startled me. He believed that, in *War and Peace*, Tolstoy neglected the plight of Russian serfs. He admired Gorky above Bunin. Among contemporary poets, he especially appreciated Akhmatova and Yesenin but did not accept Mandelstam and Pasternak. Among young authors, he praised stories by Bokov. I remember Platonov once made a remark about one place in Pasternak's poem, 'The High Malady', where he wrote of a railway station during the Communist War, "... competing in its wild beauty with the emptiness of The Musical Conservatoire on rest-days and holidays."[1] Platonov said, "A writer, concerned about the reader, compares an unknown with a little-known or well-known. Pasternak does the opposite: a station – familiar to millions of people – is likened to The Conservatoire at the time of a vacation. And how many people have seen The Conservatoire at that time?"

I responded that Pasternak looks at the empty Conservatoire with the eyes of a man familiar with its daily life. Platonov didn't take my point.

I read Voloshin's poem 'A Poet's House' to him, which pleased him. He responded to it thoughtfully, "To be a notebook, not a book, through life." When someone read him a poem, he didn't speak other than to repeat a phrase he liked several times, and in his mouth, it would take on special significance and meaning. In this way, he repeated a line from one of my poems, "trod their own path," which made me realize that in these words and with those of Voloshin[2], he heard something of the suffering of his own life.

When Grossman read us a chapter from the novel *For A Just Cause*, Platonov didn't speak either. After the reading, he repeated the expressions that had become ingrained in his soul,

---

1 +Translated by Robert Payne.
2 +Maximilian Voloshin (1877-1932), Russian poet and critic, known for his involvement in the Symbolist movement.

for example: "At Ease! Expletives!"[1] or "... Dead meat – then ceased to exist." The latter referred to a phrase about the driver who heard " ... a rising bomb wail, pressed his head against the steering wheel, felt with all his body the end of life; and thought with a sharp sense of yearning, 'Dead meat' – then ceased to exist."

I heard Platonov read two of his works. One was his wonderful *Dzhan.*[2] In this book, he described with biblical simplicity and color a small tribe who roamed the desert in the Soviet times and told a story about a soldier returning to the wife who had betrayed him while he was at the front. Platonov was the first to laugh at the funny passages.

I don't remember Platonov ever being prolix; he'd just make a guttural sound, speak softly to himself or press his lips together, and in doing so, seemed to me more profound and perceptive than any of us no matter what we said. He got to the heart of things in a concise and vivid way. He once described a literary controversy as "The blind having sex in stinging nettles."

We met at Platonov's that night in July 1943. Grossman and I had managed to get exchange coupons for vodka. We drank out of crystal glasses, and I picked up a piece of sausage that we'd got from American army rations. Platonov, deciding I'd taken more than my fair share, said I was "snacking sadistically."

One day, some time after the War ended, we went to see Platonov, and Grossman teased him, saying, "Andryusha, how come you haven't been scolded in the press for a while?" To which Platonov answered, "They think I'm convalescing like the others now." That day we talked about the current deluge of talentless and unprofessional publications that were now everywhere and Platonov said, "The reader's begun to impinge

---

1   +In the original, "Otstavit' materki!," the humorous effect stems from the combination of military lexic 'Otstavit' - as you were - and 'materki' - a funny colloquial derivative of 'mat', Russian obscene jargon.

2   +*Soul*, translated by Robert Chandler (The Harvill Press, 2003).

on literature."

I remember only one extended utterance of Platonov's on literature. He said that not every obsequious word pleases the authorities: it has to be written at the right time. It is no good if it is written too late, and it often causes anger if it is written too early: the authorities cannot stand writers who jump the gun.

Another of Platonov's traits that has remained in my memory is that he was unshockable, even by the most surprising or absurd news, whether relating to the literary or political sphere. In response to such news, he always calmly uttered the same phrase about life being "a free thing."

The Platonovs used to have rather an unusual visitor, Mikhail Sholokhov.[1] Apparently, he understood Platonov's significance, sometimes asserted it, and obtained literary work for him. Maria Alexandrovna, Platonov's wife, was very proud of this acquaintance. She was a beautiful woman who Andrei Bely described as "cold and evil." Much in her character was foreign both to Grossman and me. But her commitment to Platonov's talent was absolute. Maria Alexandrovna considered her husband superior to all other writers and felt he'd been inadequately recognized. Such dedication in a writer's wife should be acknowledged.

None of us, except Platonov, knew Sholokhov, and when Grossman asked, "Tell me, what is he like? Is he smart?" Platonov remained inscrutable, and his quiet utterances were undecipherable. Grossman always took a keen interest in Sholokhov. He felt that Sholokhov's novel *And Quiet Flows the Don* was excellent but that his *Virgin Soil Upturned* was mediocre. He considered Sholokhov very disappointing when he appeared in public.

When we met at Platonov's Herzen Street flat, I described how, at the end of February 1943, a member of the Military Council of our Fleet took me to Kamyshin. I had to do a

---

1   +Mikhail Alexandrovich Sholokhov (1915-1984), won Lenin, Stalin and Nobel prizes for his social realist novels.

story for my newspaper about a ceremony at which seriously wounded sailors who were being treated in Kamyshin naval hospital received their medals. Local residents told me that Colonel Sholokhov and his family had lived there throughout the War in a large house formerly owned by a merchant. Sholokhov received a respectful invitation to the ceremony and was given the floor after the medals were distributed. The soldiers, their eyes blinded, limbs maimed or gone, waited eagerly to hear their favorite Russian author speak to them. In the tense silence, Sholokhov proposed the following toast: "Here's to the Soviet Ukraine." And said not another word. Grossman, surprised, asked me, "Are you sure that was all he said?" then continued, "a mysterious man." Platonov spoke softly: "Words rarely come from the heart, more often from the head."

They loved each other; the hounded Platonov, whose name for a long time meant nothing to the general mass of readers, and Grossman, who was a board member of the Writers' Union during the war, well-known and recognized by the State. They had a lot in common. Both despised what State hacks called literature. And even in those writers who they admired, even in their friends, they could not tolerate half-truths, showing off, verbiage and equivocation.

However, Grossman, not only in his writing but also in his tastes, whether they related to literature, fine art, or music, was more committed to the traditions of Russian and Western European classics of the nineteenth and early twentieth century. Platonov was more independent in his judgments. Both felt drawn to workers and peasants. In Grossman, this emanated from the Social Democratic views of his youth and possibly from his father, Semyon Osipovich's Menshevik sympathies. In Platonov, the attraction to the common man stemmed from his worship of the simplest manifestations of life both in nature and in human society.

I remember the glee with which Platonov described working

with machines: "When a locomotive is in working order, you are flying, the earth and sky rush upon you, and you are the master of the whole space of the world." Neither Grossman nor Platonov believed in God, but neither ever laughed at my religious feelings, unlike many of my peers. I would say that both subscribed to materialist philosophy; Grossman, at least until that time, considered himself a Marxist, while Platonov's materialism was pantheistic, something close to the views of Fedorov.[1]

I told Grossman and Platonov about a story I'd translated from the Mahabharata in which some of the pious, traveling to an Indian shrine, see cow dung on the ground. They rush to the river to wash to avoid their pilgrimage being sullied as the god Indra materializes from the dung and castigates the pilgrims saying, "It was I who turned myself into dung – nothing in the world of creation is pure or impure." Grossman said, "Interesting." And Platonov repeated slowly, "Nothing in the world of creation is pure or impure."

I will conclude this comparison of the two men by saying that while both loved to drink, Platonov was indifferent to food while Grossman loved it. Also, Platonov, who was usually short of money, would drink with anyone who paid, even if he happened to be a dirty Black Hundredist man.[2] This enraged Grossman, who chose his drinking partners with care, demanded a lot of himself, and asserted his demands of his friends firmly; he'd shout at Platonov while looking at him lovingly. And Platonov, in his turn, reciprocated the warmth of Grossman's gaze.

After the War, we three sometimes sat on Tverskoy Boulevard, opposite Platonov's windows. A favorite pastime

---

1 +Nikolai Fedorov (1828-1903), Russian Orthodox Christian Philosopher who embraced Cosmism.

2 +Refers to member of the ultranationalist Black Hundreds founded in the early 20th century which supported the Romanovs, Russocentric doctrine denial of Ukranian nationality, anti-semitsm and the incitement of pogroms.

was making up stories about passers-by who caught our attention. Leaving me or my insipid accounts aside, Grossman and Platonov were each graphically characterized by theirs. Grossman's were detailed. If he thought someone looked like an accountant, he'd add that they kept books at a candy factory. If he thought someone seemed like a tradesman, he'd say he headed the electricity plant. Then there'd be portraits of his wife, children and old drunk father who was a peasant from Mozhaisk; Grossman always included so much humor and sadness. Platonov's stories were quite different. There were no plots; they described man's thoughts and feelings. They were unusual and at the same time as simple as the depiction of the life of a plant.

We once sat on Tverskoy during the brutal campaign against 'cosmopolitanism.' Grossman went to the tobacco kiosk at the corner when Ivan Nikanorovich Rozanov[1], a nice old man who was a professor and a fan of poetry, shuffled to our bench. He smiled broadly, showed his long, widely spaced teeth and said, "Do you feel how the air's cleared of the smell of garlic?" Then he walked away, tapping on his cane. It seemed the old man had forgotten that both Grossman and I were Jews. When Grossman returned with his cigarettes, I told him what had happened. Grossman was taken aback at first, then said, "Nice old man!" and proceeded to shout at both Platonov and me, rebuking us for not reacting to the insult, asking why had we just swallowed it up? As he raged, Platonov kept saying languidly, "Come on, Vasya," and looked confused. In *Life and Fate*, Rozanov's comment is put in the mouth of the old teacher.

Platonov contracted tuberculosis from his poor dying son,

---

1 +Ivan Rozanov (1874-1959), headed Moscow's historical museum's department of the history of books from 1919-1941 and from 1945-1953 worked at the Gorky Institute of World Literature of the USSR's Academy of Sciences. He published 300 books including *Russian Lyric Poetry* (1914), *Songs by Russian Poets* (1936), and *Nineteenth Century Russian Songs* (1944) and collected a unique library of Russian poetry now housed in Moscow's Pushkin Museum. His medals included the Red Banner of Labor.

whom he'd kissed on the lips in a frenzy. Grossman visited
Platonov's sick bed almost every day. I once went with him. I'll
never forget the sharp gleam, the linger of anguish in Platonov's
sunken eyes, thin yellow face and persistent quiet cough.
As he wrote to me, Platonov's death shocked and exhausted
Grossman after attending to Platonov's funeral arrangements
which he'd dealt with "because none at the Writers' Union had
undertaken to settle them."

I remember the heartfelt eulogy that Grossman delivered
for his friend in the presence of the few who came to honor
Platonov's memory from the Writers' Union (a group that
thinned even further in the small clean Armenian cemetery
opposite the Vagan'kovsky cemetery when we later buried
Platonov). Grossman's speech gave a clever and wry description
of the precious writer who died underrated in virtual obscurity.
This speech could not be published for a long time. In January
1960, Grossman wrote to me:

> The people from the Radio Committee offered me
> the opportunity to speak on the radio about Andrei
> Platonov. I agreed and wrote a short article.
> Let's see if anything comes of this. Perhaps my
> luck will improve when I embrace the akyn's genre.[1]

The article based on the funeral speech was read by
Grossman on the radio, and it became the first intelligent,
sensible, and decent word spoken publically in Russia about
Platonov. *Literary Russia* published the article when they
reviewed a book of Platonov's which appeared after his
death. At a time when very little was known about Platonov,
Grossman wrote:

> He was a writer who wished to examine the most
> complex, and therefore the simplest, basic principles
> of human existence.

---

1   +Akyns are improvising poets, singers and eulogizers.

An amazing formula, mathematically short and striking in its depth and elegance. Grossman led his search in a different way, but both were looking for the same thing, and it was not accidental that Grossman said of his friend, "Platonov would not write if he were not looking for the human in man, looking tirelessly, frantically, and unrestrainedly, always and everywhere."

Until the end of his life, Grossman did not stop remembering Platonov, reading and re-reading him. In one of his later letters, he wrote to me:

> I read Platonov's stories. What a gigantic strength they have: 'Takyr', 'The Third Son', 'Fro.' You feel as if you hear a voice of a friend in the desert, both joyful and bitter. The man wrote a book, and this is a serious matter.

In 1943 Grossman began the novel *For A Just Cause*. I remember he told me about this after he had experienced a tragedy. His family had been evacuated to Christopol, and his elder stepson, Misha, was called up there by the Chistopol draft office for pre-training when a bomb exploded in the courtyard of the draft office, and Misha was killed. He was not yet sixteen years old. Olga told me that their neighbor in Christopol, Boris Pasternak, dug the grave and did it very skillfully. With his help, they found a priest in that Tatar city and buried the boy in accordance with the Russian Orthodox rite. Olga Mikhailovna's sorrow lives on the pages of *Life and Fate*, where Shtrum's wife Lyudmila (she's generally based on Olga) arrives in Saratov to visit her son's grave after he dies in hospital as a result of heavy wounds.

Grossman built his *For A Just Cause* like a commander builds an army. We see rapid deployment of heroes, flash-like focuses on individual plots, maneuvering and mobility of storylines, verbal counterattacks and breakthroughs on the flanks and speedy actions of motorized weaponry of phrases and pictures. It's no accident that some well-known young writers – who some might call avant-garde – admire the design of both *For A Just Cause* and *Life and Fate*.

The author not only doesn't hide but deliberately emphasizes the similarity of plans of *For A Just Cause* and *War and Peace*. Tolstoy puts the Rostov family at the center of his novel, Grossman, the Shaposhnikovs. Tolstoy speaks and thinks for the author; Grossman does this for Shtrum. If the Rostov family is biographically close to Tolstoy's, Shaposhnikov's sisters embody Olga and her sisters. And from Tolstoy's thoughts about the "cudgel of people's war" stems Grossman's thought that in Stalingrad's fateful hours, it wasn't:

> Russia's slavery and death that were born in the blood
> and scolded stone mist ... but the force of Soviet man,
> which stubbornly endured, subsisted, emerged.

Grossman's deliberate parallels with *War and Peace* continued and were fully achieved not in *For A Just Cause* but in *Life and Fate*, Grossman's supreme achievement. Nevertheless, *For A Just Cause* remains one of the most important novels of the Soviet period of Russian literature.

Even before the release of *Life and Fate* as a separate publication, foreign readers of the magazine, *Vremia i my* (*Time and Us*), could read a chapter of the novel.[1] The chosen chapter was strong and important. The introductory article by Yefim Etkind[2] was intelligent and sensible in my view. Excellent, I would say. Future readers will thank Simon Markish[3] (son of the poet Peretz Markish) and Etkind for the huge and challenging endeavor they undertook to publish the novel in full. Etkind's preface to the separate publication is also commendable. But

---

1   +*Time and Us* (1976), first appeared in Tel Aviv and later in New York.
2   +Yefim Etkind (1918-1999), Soviet philologist and translation theorist who left Russia in 1974 and lived in Paris.
3   +Simon Markish (1931-2003), Soviet literary historian who left Russia in 1970 and lived in Geneva.

in the anonymous note "From the Publisher" that prefaced the novel, there is one passage with which I cannot agree. The author maintains that prior to *Life and Fate*, Grossman was a prosperous Soviet writer and notes that *For A Just Cause* was no better than *White Birch* by Bubennov[1]. He wrote that:

> *For A Just Cause* is an ordinary novel of Stalin's era, on a par with Bubennov's *White Birch* and Simonov's *Day and Night*.

I feel it necessary to object strongly and decisively to this view. First of all, Grossman was not a prosperous Soviet writer. He was in literary demand for a short period during the War years, just like intelligent, brave, and skillful soldiers and officers were in demand during that time.

Writers died on the battlefield and deserve tribute. Whereas many who'd professed their heroism and readiness to go to the front hid in the rear, the modest, short-sighted Grossman and the persecuted Platonov did their military service with talent and courage.

But the War wasn't over when Grossman's essay 'The Ukraine Without Jews' angered the authorities.[2] And his play *If You Believe the Pythagoreans*[3] published shortly after the War, was part of the painful, fearful and long path of the novel, *For A Just Cause*. During this period, Grossman and I hid at my dacha in Ilyinskoye, where each gust of night wind, each tap of the shutters, or step in the empty street caused us to say, "They're coming after us."

His book, with its realistic portraits of ordinary people, peasants, workers, oppressed women, the bitter truths

---

1   +Mikhail Semyonovich Bubennov (1909-1983), Soviet writer and journalist.

2   +Initially rejected for publication in 1943 by *The Red Star*. Then translated into Yiddish and partially published in the weekly paper of the Jewish Anti-Facist Committee, *Einikayt* (*Unity*).

3   +*If you Believe the Pythagoreans*, Vasily Grossman, trans. Polly Zaradivker (published 1946).

of everyday Soviet life, its brilliant description of Hitler, Stalingrad's fire, the Filyashkin battalion's destruction, and of how Major Berezkin met his wife, was no ordinary novel. How can it be compared to the banal, now-forgotten *Day and Night* or *White Birch*? And would an ordinary Soviet novel attract such heavy blows which nearly destroyed both it and its author?

It must be said if the characters of the novel written by a creative pen are meted out for a long life, the arguments of the author will never be accepted by all readers. *For A Just Cause* was written at the time of a radical turn in The Patriotic War. The Germans, who had hoisted the swastika flag on Mount Elbrus, were driven back by the Red Army, who freed Russian, Belorussian, and Ukrainian villages and towns. Grossman, the artist, decided to answer the question, "How could this turn happen during the War?" The answer he gave was:

> The victors were people who were brought up with, and lived believing in, the international equality of workers; the winners were workers and peasants who had become rulers of Russia. Besides, an axe raised over us by the enemy was an axe raised over human faithfulness to freedom, over a dream for justice, a joy of labor, over loyalty to the Motherland.

In Grossman's opinion, the High Command knew about the "already existing moral superiority of Soviet force over German violence." With that in mind, Grossman began writing his novel. Emphasizing the view of the High Command, he did not think then that we were led by the Almighty.

Once, in the fifties, long before the events in Hungary, we had lunch at the barbecue restaurant in Gorky Park. Slightly drunk, we started arguing about the War. A dispute flared up between us and we ran like crazy through the Park's alleys, each shouting our heads off. Finally, exhausted, we sat down on a bench but continued the argument and only came round when we saw a man sitting next to us listening. We got scared and sobered up.

Among the heroes of Grossman's war essays was Colonel (later Marshal of the Armored Forces) Babajanyan, with whom Grossman kept up an acquaintance that had started during the War. I did not know him, but during our argument made some assumptions about how he and people like him would have behaved in an emergency. Shortly after our crazy dispute, Grossman learned that Babajanyan participated in the suppression of the Hungarian uprising. Grossman rang me up and said, "Come out" (we were neighbors in Begovaya Street), and, without explanation, he said into the phone, "You've just looked into water."[1]

I return to the book *For A Just Cause*. From the first pages of the novel, Soviet readers learn things that the State's writers never talk about. An old peasant Pukhov believes that the State always rests on the peasant and the State is heavy. Peasant life, he maintains, is worse than under the Tsar, and he concludes: "Anything but the collective farms." With a sympathy unthinkable among the Soviet writers of Stalin's time, Grossman writes about the repression of "enemies of the people," about old Shaposhnikova's son Dmitri, about Abarchuk and the dispossessed kulaks, working at a construction site alongside Komsomol members, "the frost is the same for everyone ... there were gullies, dust, barracks and barbed wire." You cannot read descriptions like this of construction sites in the works of any other Soviet writer; Mayakovsky's hints are all there are.[2] Mayakovsky glorified the construction site when he said, "I know the city will be,"[3] but the pastoral of the leader and agitator mentions neither repressed people nor barbed wire.

In the bunker, amid the rumble of explosions, roar of

---

1   +Read the future.

2   +*People From The Back Woods* by Aleksander Malyshkin (Raduga, 1984).

3   +A quote from 'At The Top Of My Voice', 1930, Mayakovsky's last uncompleted poem.

missiles and clatter of anti-aircraft fire, the personnel director asks Lieutenant Colonel Darensky where his wife is, and Darensky knows nothing about his wife because he was in prison before the War. I could probably cite hundreds of such passages, but when all is said and done, the heart of the matter is not in them but in the fact that *For A Just Cause* was alien to socialist realism. The novel contradicted it by its entire vocabulary, its music, its painting and its close attention to the detail of everyday life and human relations, all the things bureaucratic Soviet literature deliberately ignored. It contradicted socialist realism by its forms of argument (argument beyond the statutory, even in a Marxist vein, was discouraged and seen as a provocation), but ultimately in its originality and spontaneity of true talent. On the other hand, sometimes you read works written from a non-Soviet perspective and see that not only their verbal shell but their composition bursting with socialist realism.

Among the few failures of *For A Just Cause*, I want to focus on one character; the Old Bolshevik Mostovsky. Later, in *Life and Fate*, Mostovsky becomes flesh and blood in his meeting in the German concentration camp with the one-eyed Menshevik (incidentally, Grossman's father, Semyon Osipovich, was one-eyed). However, in the novel *For A Just Cause*, Mostovsky's remarks seem to me vapid, and his optimism sounds tedious. But this is not as simple as it sounds. Stalin persecuted Old Bolsheviks, and he destroyed their Society and drove them out of their homes.[1] Many were shot or tortured in penal servitude. So when Grossman portrays Mostovsky as an educated pre-revolutionary Bolshevik with firm ideological principles, he challenges Stalin. It has to be said that Grossman's powers of observation never fail him. Mostovsky decides to stay in German-occupied Stalingrad and boasts about his previous experience as a conspirator. However, he is instantly seized by

---

1   +The All Union Society of Old Bolsheviks.

the Germans, irrespective of the fact he's done nothing. War nullifies and makes void the entirety of Mostovsky's Bolshevik experience.

Grossman often deploys what Turgenev, speaking of Dostoevsky, called "a reverse commonplace." Mostovsky is an example of this, as is Sokolova, the kindergarten nurse. She is a heavy drinker, a defendant in criminal proceedings but it is she who, by her love, restores to health Grisha Serpokryl, a boy whose brain is clouded after his father and mother are killed in an air raid. Krymov, too: no matter how orthodox his views are, the reader is worried by something in him, and throughout the whole of this vast novel, those misgivings persist.

Inevitably, the novel (at first called *Stalingrad*) was rejected by Simonov[1], the Editor in Chief of *Novy Mir*[2], and by his deputy Krivitsky.[3] They took a year to make their decision which left Grossman anxious. He was so earnest and serious about his work; it was so important to him. He seemed to sink into an abyss. Finally, the answer came: *Novy Mir* could not print *Stalingrad*. But just after Simonov returned the novel to Grossman, there was a replacement on the editorial board. Tvardovsky[4] was appointed chief editor of the Journal, and the critic Tarasenkov[5] was appointed his deputy. Tarasenkov was the first to read the novel, and, enraptured, he made a late-night phone call to Grossman. Then Tvardovsky read it, and concurred with his deputy. Both came to Grossman's flat in the Begovaya. Tvardovsky sincerely and solemnly congratulated Grossman; there were hugs, kisses, and drunken

---

1 +Konstantin Simonov (1915-1979), poet, playwrite, novelist.

2 +[*New World*], the official organ of the Writers' Union.

3 +In 1958 Krivitstky laid down guidelines for how authors were able to treat previously taboo tragic themes: "Draw us a zebra - black stripe, bright stripe, black stripe, bright stripe. Step back and you've got an objective picture." Page 221, *Soviet Fictions Since Stalin*, Rosalind Marsh (Barnes and Noble, 1986).

4 +Aleksander Tvardovsky (1910-1971), poet who fought hard to maintain *Novy Mir*'s independent publishing of Ehrenberg and Solzhenitsyn.

5 +Anatoly Tarasenkov (1917-1978).

tears. The decision was made to print the novel and, once Tvardovsky composed himself, he raised three serious objections. Firstly, the portrayal of war and the difficulty of killing throughout were too graphic and grim. Secondly, too little was said about Stalin. And thirdly, its Jewish theme; one of the main characters, physicist Shtrum was Jewish, and the doctor, Sofia Levinton, so warmly depicted, was Jewish. "Why not make Shtrum a head of a Voentorg,"[1] advised Tvardovsky. Grossman's angry retort was, "And what role would you suggest for Einstein?"

Tvardovsky loved the role and responsibility of being an editor. He made a lot of useful notes on the margins of the manuscript. Among other things, he noted the following: Krymov in the novel was initially named Krylov, and there already was another character with this name, General Krylov, an actual historical person, Chief of Staff of the 62nd Army. So Tvardovsky advised Krylov should be changed to Krymov; he said altering just one letter would facilitate the edit.

Tvardovsky felt eager to publish *Stalingrad* and was convinced that the author would agree to the amendments, which would neutralize objections. He acted with deliberation and looked for support. He posted the novel to Sholokhov, who was on the editorial board of *Novy Mir*. Tvardovsky hoped that the "great Soviet writer" could not but be attracted by the artistic merits of *Stalingrad* and support its artistic value with his immense authority despite the rumor he didn't like its author. I saw Sholokhov's brief response, a few typewritten lines that, as I recall it, essentially amounted to:

Who have you commissioned to write about the battle of Stalingrad? Do you know what you are doing? I oppose it.

Grossman and I were particularly struck by the phrase:

---

1   +A military shop.

"Who have you commissioned ..." and its wildly bureaucratic approach to literature.

Tvardovsky held his course, was steadfast and obstinate and appealed for help to Fadeyev, who led the Writers' Union. He needed that kind of support because the novel had influential opponents at different levels of the state machine. Fadeyev read the novel very quickly and agreed with Tvardovsky that it should be published.

A gray-haired member of the Party Central Committee came to Grossman one evening and stayed late into the night, saying to him affectionately, "What a bright spark you are," intimating that he admired his artist's spirit. Copies of *Stalingrad* were made and distributed to the members of the Writers' Union's Secretariat. When they met, Fadeyev was in charge, and Grossman was invited. The reports were that every member except one (I don't remember who it was) praised the book. Firstly, it was decided to recommend that *Novy Mir* publish it. Secondly, that its title should be changed from *Stalingrad* so that no single author monopolized the greatest battle as subject matter (since the "anti-cosmopolitan" campaign, the subtext was clear.) Thirdly, Shtrum should have a superior, a teacher, a much greater physicist, and an ethnic Russian. Fourthly, Grossman should write a chapter on Stalin.

Grossman accepted all these proposals, and other minor ones as he had no choice. When he asked me what I thought, I said that one had to agree but for me it would be repugnant to write about Stalin. Grossman got angry. "How many poems about the leader have you translated?"

I quoted my father's saying, "You can go to a brothel, but don't confuse it with a synagogue." Grossman responded with words from an Armenian joke, "Go teach yourself."

The novel was met by filthy attacks, covert and overt, from literary and supra-literary forces. Tvardovsky and Fadeyev did not give up, and Grossman, of course, seeing them as his protectors, was ready to meet them halfway. He wrote a chapter about Stalin and tried to portray him with a human face without adopting the generally accepted cosmic comparisons. He also introduced a new character into the novel, an outstanding scientist, Chepyzhin, as Shtrum's teacher.

Fadeyev, who had previously been cold and suspicious. perhaps even hostile to Grossman, met him several times in his apartment. He understood the literary importance of Grossman's novel. They started talking, in front of me, about a title. *Stalingrad*, as I mentioned earlier, wasn't acceptable. At that time, an official critic had praised Popovkin's work, *The Family Rubanyuk*. This title amused Grossman somehow, and he suggested angrily, "I will name the novel, *The Family Rubanyuk*. Fadeyev's cheerful, childish laugh resounded as he said, "Yes, yes, call it something like 'Family Rubanyuk.'" During this conversation, it was decided to call the novel *For A Just Cause* (an expression from a speech Molotov delivered on the first day of the war). I don't remember who suggested it, whether it was Fadeyev or Grossman himself.

Both Fadeyev's unexpectedly positive attitude to the novel and his subsequent betrayal are easy to explain. Fadeyev loved Russian literature with all his heart (and he had a heart). He could not bear the literary trash flooding us at that time, but he had to remain in power by publicly praising what he really thought was incompetence. Maybe the reader will better understand Fadeyev's personality – which left its mark on that entire literary era – if I focus on one episode.

At the end of the war, my family lived in such an incredible crush that in winter, to have a place to work, I settled with Nikolai Chukovsky in a half-empty cottage in Peredelkino[1] (this was before I had the dacha in Ilyinskoye). It belonged to his father (the notable Soviet writer Korney Chukovsky).

We were friends with Nikolai Zabolotsky[2], who returned

---

1   +Writers' colony outside Moscow.
2   +Nikolai Zabolotsky (1903-1958), a metaphysical poet and member of OBERIU (Union of Real Art).

from exile in Karaganda and found refuge nearby. We often got together. Now and then, Fadeyev came in the evening to read us excerpts from the novel he was finishing that winter called *Young Guard*. Sometimes during his drinking fits he became surprisingly human. He once said, "What's going on in our literature is the end of the world. I received a story, *Cavalier of Gold Star*[1] sent from Pyatigorsk; someone upstairs liked it, dear Kolyas and Syoma[2]. It beats everything; all I can do is issue an SOS call." Then he recited, with feeling and heart, Pasternak's 'Deep Blue Colour'[3], then scenes from Gogol's 'A Terrible Vengeance', then 'I Go Out Alone On The Road'[4], and did them all very well.

One day I found myself invited to a meeting of The Writers' Union's Presidium on Books nominated for the Stalin Prize. As Chairman of the Kyrgyz Literature Commission, I had to report to The Presidium about a Kyrgyz poet's book. As I sat and waited for my author's book's turn, *The Cavalier of Gold Star* by Babayevsky was announced and applauded. Fadeyev took the podium, praised Babayevsky, and suddenly, turning to me and fixing me with his wolf-blue eyes, he said maliciously, "There still remain snobs who turn their noses up at stories like these." No one understood why Fadeyev looked at me because my role that day was minimal, my speciality narrow, and I hadn't even read Babayevsky. Fadeyev must have remembered how he'd derided this "cavalier" in front of me, grown angry with himself, and decided to visit his wrath on me.

Eventually, all obstacles were overcome and Grossman's novel was published in four issues of *Novy Mir*. The editorial

---

1   +This is a novel by Semyon Petrovich Babayevski (1909-2000). The novel was published in 1947 and became a symbol of paradisiacal descriptions of the world.

2   +Diminutives of Nikolai and Semyon, respectively.

3   +Actually, Nikoloz Baratashvili's poem, translated by Boris Pasternak.

4   +An old Russian romantic song, words by Mikhail Lermontov, melody by Elizaveta Shashina.

board members were nervous. Tarasenkov told Grossman, "I'll believe in our victory only when I buy the magazine at a newsstand."

In January 1950, Grossman wrote to me in Maleyevka[1]:

At *Novy Mir*, the third installment is now being typeset; tomorrow they will start giving me early proofs of the fourth and final installment. Then I can go to Koktebel[2].

There's lots of talk, but so far, there are no thorns, but they will appear according to the law of botany. What have you heard? Oh, well! You know how I feel – the main thing has been achieved. And you know, I still feel and understand that sharply and deeply, like when my short story, 'In the City of Berdichev' was first published. Perhaps even more intensely. I must tell you that I'm writing a little. You know how persistent we graphomaniacs are.

The impression the novel made was tremendous both in literary circles and amongst an intelligentsia looking for truth and poetry. It shouldn't be forgotten that it was published in the years when society ran wild, with the struggle against "cosmopolitanism," and literature and art slowly deteriorating. The quick-witted cynic Yermilov[3], editor of *Literaturnaya Gazeta*, said of that time that "Marasmus grew stronger." It had been Yermilov who'd written the crushing article in *Pravda* about Grossman's play, *If You Believe the Pythagoreans*, at a time when Moscow's Art Theater, so dear to the Russian soul, staged Surov's plays and with such success.

The witty Emmanuel Kazakevich[4] devoted a sonnet to Surov

---

1   +House for writers outside of Moscow.
2   +A house for writers on the coast of the Black Sea.
3   +Vasyl Yermilov (1894-1968), modern artist from the Ukraine.
4   +Emmanuel Kazakevich (1913-1962), author, poet and playwright of Jewish extraction, writing in Russian and Yiddish.

called, 'Severe Surov did not like the Jews.' Later they had to oust Surov from the Writers' Union in disgrace, as it was found that he lacked the talent even for his mediocre plays, which were, in fact, written by ghostwriters, some of whom were Jews.

The publication was a success. Every edition of *Novy Mir* sold out instantly, and there were long queues at libraries for them. There were enthusiastic responses in literary circles and in the press.

"The bells are peeling, and although the procession hasn't begun, we're raising the banners." Phrases like this, written by the old proletarian writer Bakhmetyev[1] and others praising the novel, later appeared in *Life and Fate* in reference to Shtrum's breakthrough in nuclear physics. The language of research, maths, and physics convey the atmosphere created in the press around *For A Just Cause*. In an article called 'The People's War Epic' (a headline that carried great weight in the Soviet press), the novel was described as "A real triumph, a classic work."

Voengiz[2] and Sovetsky Pisatel'[3] were going to publish the novel in book form, but the "Laws of Botany," mentioned in Grossman's letter, overtook events. Not just thorns but poisoned arrows and spears were shot through the novel. Remarkably, it was the character Chepyzhin, introduced by Grossman at Fadeyev's urging to "neutralize" Shtrum, who was criticized by the Party. Chepyzhin's thoughts – that society was a firmament and that in hard and dark days, all evil rises from the bottom of society – were seen as anti-Marxist.

On February 13th and 14th, 1953, *Pravda* published a two-part article by Mikhail Bubennov called "On Grossman's Novel *For A Just Cause*." The apoplectic author of the *White Birch* (which, as discussed earlier, had been compared to Grossman's novel) was consumed with the envy and malice of a rodent and

---

1   +Vladimir Matveevich Bakhmetyev (1885-1963), celebrated Soviet novelist and member of the Smiths literary group.

2   +Military state publishing house.

3   +The publishing house of the Writers' Union.

wrote, of course, what he thought himself. However, the ideas expounded by him were not just his own. He paid tribute to the knowledge of the war shown by Grossman as a participant in the Battle of Stalingrad and agreed that there were fresh, truthful chapters that portrayed the Nazi army. He approved of the scenes in the hospital, of the bombings, and of Berezkin's fortuitous meetings with his wife and daughter. After that, Bubennov quickly proceeded to his main task:

> These individual successes cannot conceal Grossman's big failure. He failed to create a single large, bright image of a typical hero of the Battle of Stalingrad, the hero in a gray overcoat, carrying a firearm ... The novel *For A Just Cause* does not present typical characters who evoke the main traits and essence of Soviet people. There are no characters in it that strike the imagination of the reader with the richness and beauty of their feelings ... the images of the Soviet people in the novel are meager, depreciated, and discolored ... the author tries to prove that immortal exploits are achieved by ordinary people, but under the guise of the ordinary, he pulls to the fore a gallery of paltry, insignificant people. Not in the least does Grossman show The Party as the organizer of the victory, either in the rear or in the army's hierarchy ... to the enormous theme of the organizing and inspiring role of The Communist Party, he ascribes only declarations ... they are not evidenced by artistic images.

When copying passages from Bubennov's article, I become filled with that dismal feeling experienced by the people of my generation who read such things in *Pravda* during Stalin's life. The feeling smells like a prison, perhaps like death. I must admit that Bubennov and his invisible co-authors clearly saw the danger that 'ordinary' – i.e., real people – constituted.

Socialist realism does not fear decadence and modernism, it persecutes them because it has to do so, but it is not afraid of them. Socialist realism fears realism. Thus The Antichrist does not fear disbelief or paganism; he can recruit them to be his brothers-in-arms. The Antichrist fears Christ.

Bubennov had a weapon in reserve, not a new weapon but one tested over centuries, and in Soviet times this weapon was deployed only in Stalin's latter years. Bubennov wrote about the relationship between the Shaposhnikov and Shtrum families, "Sofya Osipovna Levinton lives close to the family ...."

To interrupt Bubennov for a moment, Sofya Levinton is a doctor, and the fiction of 'doctor-murderers' was currently being conceived in the country. Bubennov does his best to drive the reader to the core of his message:

> This family is unremarkable and uninteresting as a Soviet family. Yet, Grossman portrays them as a typical Soviet family worthy of being at the center of the saga of Stalingrad.

Indeed, what kind of a Russian family is it? Although the name of its founder, Shaposhnikova, is a street name in Kuibyshev, the family is related to and makes friends with the Shtrums, Levintons, and an enemy of the people, Krymov, whom the monster of the human race, Trotsky, once called, "marble." Who did Grossman put in this family? Shtrum, who "thinks more than others and talks more than others about historical events." The question for Bubennov was, what kind of people was Grossman depicting?

His article continues:

> After allotting a considerable space to gray, inactive characters, Grossman, of course, could not give serious attention to the sort of characters that should have been shown in the foreground of the novel ... the heroic feat of the Soviet warriors is not faithfully

ideologically interpreted ... in a number of episodes the author persistently emphasizes motives of doom and sacrifice ... some press-published articles praise the novel without restraint ... they manifest the ideological blindness and lack of principle of some literary people tied because of bonds of friendship ... it's easy to see how much damage that does to the development of Soviet literature.

Bubennov's article was the work of a hangman. We, to our misfortune, were accustomed to the hangman's articles on literature and art, but in this case, an innovation had been introduced, and readers understood it. "Some literary people tied because of bonds of friendship ..." implied a Jewish conspiracy.

Today's hangmen may be more sly and cunning than Bubennov, but they are still there. How bitter it is that such werewolves turn the great Russian idea of human suffering, turn the land of the King of Heaven, blessed in its length and breadth, into an executioner's block. And in the name of Russia, and on its behalf, they used this block to murder beauty whether created by Levitan, Mandelstam, Pasternak, or Grossman. They bring more and more harm to our country, but they number only a handful. People with hearts and minds will outweigh them.

As recently as 1970, Anatoly Bocharov released a critical bibliographical essay called 'Grossman.' The fact that he did so deserves respect and appreciation. On one of the last pages of this rather voluminous book Bochorov writes:

Grossman became increasingly intransigent, intolerant, and forthright, but as his character strengthened, he suffered the pain of loneliness.

Bochorov is alluding to the period after *Life and Fate* was arrested, when Grossman got cancer. But Grossman's character began changing earlier than that with the start of the destruction of *For A Just Cause*. And it was not Grossman's forthrightness that drove him to the pain of loneliness, but his friends who were afraid of it and who left him alone at a difficult time. In *Life and Fate*, Grossman describes with sad accuracy what he went through. Shtrum, the agoraphobic, reluctant to cross public squares, is Grossman's alter ego of whom it's said:

> It was as though everyone suddenly became profoundly short-sighted. Friends approached him, then walked straight past. Thoughtful but quiet … he kept a count of the nods, handshakes … daily visitors, which became rare, and then stopped.

Grossman did not know that more grief was yet to come – the arrest of *Life and Fate* when he would be abandoned by almost everyone. For now, he still had a few friends, but some irritated him; he felt they were selfish, cold, preoccupied with purposeless worry, and deliberate in their refusal to understand the scale of his concerns. He was right in many instances. During his early career, a critic had praised his stories, and although the critic actually wasn't very literary or knowledgeable, he was a deeply honest and fearless man who kept visiting Grossman even when he was persona non grata. When Grossman asked how he was, he naively answered, "I've got trouble, too, the article I sent to *Uchitel'skaya Gazeta*[1] hasn't been published, and it's been a whole month."

Grossman got angry and kicked his friend out on his ear. It was so silly to compare a tiny commissioned article with *Life and Fate*, which the whole imperial establishment had crushed. There'd been no malice, but the thoughtlessness sickened Grossman to his soul and made his wound bleed.

But Grossman wasn't in limbo. He had friends, his favorites

---

1   +The Teachers Newspaper.

being Boris Yampolsky[1], Viktor Nekrasov, and the literary critic Nikolai Bogoslovsky. Nikolai was a childlike believer and a pure man. On Begovaya street, we, the neighbors, formed a close circle, Grossman, Zabolotsky, Stepanov (a professor of philology), and I. Nikolai Chukovsky would come to visit but later, Grossman and I stopped seeing him.

One day Grossman decided to forget the impending dark by, as he put it, "making a little feast during the plague." He suggested that we write each other's biographies making sure to include comic memories, of course, "Material for future academic and encyclopedic studies." Zabolotsky's piece on Grossman was the funniest. He told a story of how they both walked around Moscow. Grossman noticed everything, every detail, every pebble, every garment, but when they got home, Zabolotsky said, The solar eclipse is over now, Grossman."

"Oh," his friend answered, "Was there one?"

Zabolotsky told it much better than I've done here, and Grossman split his sides laughing. I don't know what happened to those biographies.

We visited my mother almost every Sunday. She loved cooking us traditional Jewish foods, and Grossman loved eating them. It was Mikhoels[2] who defined the trait of 'gastronomic patriotism.' Grossman was very close to my mother; he knew how to talk to her. He generally knew how to talk to people, whether peasants, cleaners, or eminent physicists. I felt he made everyone feel special, although they might have no idea who they were speaking to. My mother liked him,

---

1   +Boris Yampolsky (1912–1972), Soviet writer and editor.
2   +Solomon Mikhoels (1890–1948), a Soviet Jewish actor and the artistic director of the Moscow State Jewish Theater. Mikhoels served as the chairman of the Jewish Anti-Fascist Committee during the Second World War. However, as Joseph Stalin pursued an increasingly anti-Semitic line after the War, Mikhoels' position as a leader of the Jewish community led to increasing persecution from the Soviet state. In 1948, Mikhoels was murdered on the orders of Stalin and his body was run over to create the impression of a traffic accident.

and not just because he was a talented and famous writer. He understood the grief she felt at having lost a daughter in infancy, talked to her knowledgeably about cooking particular dishes, and engaged her on the subject of the neighbors in the communal apartment. Some of what they discussed found its way into his work.

He and I would go to cafés and restaurants. I remember one funny story – well, a mildly amusing one – about a night we could not get into our usual haunts, The National, Astoria, or Aragvi hotels, because they had conferences on and so were closed to ordinary citizens. We tried to get into The Metropol, where we had never been before, and they let us in, but the tables were full, except one by the door where a short, dark, thick-set man was sitting. The waiter brought our order fast, and we raised our glasses to the chap and began to knock them back. Suddenly a big fat man came across the room, twirled one of his index fingers around the other in front of his stomach, and began a sober taunt "Little Jews, big paunches, little Jews, big paunches." With the merest flick, the chap on our table stood up and floored our big fat assailant, who rolled away over The Metropol's strip of red carpet. A wary silence ensued; the man was hauled to his feet and staggered off. It turned out when we spoke to the chap on our table that he was a prize athlete, Grigory Novak[1]. We'd thought The Metropol would have stopped those taunts, but as Grossman said to Novak, "What you did was the only way to respond."

Everywhere the dregs of society were surging. Bubennov's article on *For A Just Cause* (so evidently dictated) wasn't alone. Other attacks were even more vitriolic and frightening. It was rumored, fairly accurately, that *For A Just Cause* angered Malenkov, who was Stalin's closest functionary. Marietta

---

1 +Weight Lifting World Champion in 1946, Silver Medalist in 1952 at the Olympic Games in Helsinki.

Shaginyan, nicknamed 'self-seeking Shaginyan,[1]' wrote a disparaging article in *Izvestiya* [*The News*]. Fadeyev came forward with a short, powerful final blow. Tvardovsky reversed the authorization for the novel's publication at the Writers' Union Secretariat's meeting, recanted its publication in his journal, and his editorial board renounced the novel in the press. Grossman himself was also forced to recant, and his circle dwindled.

At that time, I was also shunned, but I never compared my situation to Grossman's. I found myself accused of promoting Bey-feudalism through two Turkic epics I translated, *Manas* and *Idegey*, and of promoting deported Kalmyks by translating their epic *Jangar*. I came before The Writers' Union Secretariat, where Fadeyev and Simonov defended me (the latter at Grossman's request). Ostensibly it ended in a reprimand, but its true end was unknowable. My good friends Samuel Galkin and Peretz Markish, Jewish poets who I had translated, were arrested, while on trams, buses, and trains, people read about doctors who were murderers, and Jewish pharmacists who sold drugs that infected people with syphilis.

Grossman and I decided at this point that it would be best if we both hid at my dacha in Ilyinskoye on the Kazan Railway line. Our routine involved me shopping for provisions in the nearby town of Zhukovsky (which was easy) and washing the dishes, whereas Grossman prepared the same good, nourishing soup for our daily lunch.

One day Fadeyev phoned and said Grossman should come over to his home immediately because Olga Mikhailovna was coming to visit with him. She was very excited, and Grossman left on an early morning train. Unfortunately, all I remember of the conversation Grossman later relayed to me is that, in Tvardovsky's words, he was told to "… repent publically and renounce *For A Just Cause* for as long as he lived on this earth."

---

1   +Marietta Shaginyan (1888-1982), Symbolist writer who adopted the methods of Socialist Realism.

Grossman refused. A tiny detail stays with me; Grossman reported that Fadeyev had puffed out his cheeks when he saw him because he was surprised he'd put on weight as a result of our nourishing lunches at the dacha.

Before we'd left for Ilyinskoye, something had happened to Grossman, which we often later remembered painfully. He'd been invited to *Pravda* by Isaac Izrailevich Mintz, a professor of history, who'd telephoned and said he must come to the editorial office to discuss the fate of the Jewish people. On the way there, Grossman had visited *Novy Mir*. He'd wanted to get his relationship with Tvardovsky clear in his mind now that Tvardovsky had abjured *For A Just Cause*. As far as I could tell from Grossman's account, the exchange had been very rough and sharp. Among other things, Tvardovsky had said, "Do you want me to risk my Party card?" "I do," Grossman replied. Tvardovsky had flushed with rage and said, "I know where you should go from here. Go on. You probably don't realize things yet; they'll explain them to you at *Pravda*."

Pravda had gathered distinguished writers, scientists, artists, and actors of Jewish origin and asked them to sign a letter drafted by Mintz to Stalin. The letter called the Doctors[1] vile murderers and said they should be subject to the most severe penalties. The letter continued by saying that the Jewish people as a whole were not to blame and that there were many honest workers and Soviet patriots among them. According to Grossman, the cartoonist Yefimov[2], the brother of murdered and repressed journalist Mikhail Kolstov, spoke in particularly offensive terms. The letter was never sent to Stalin, nor was it conceived at the highest echelons of power. The well-informed Ilya Ehrenburg explained this to us later. It was the idea of Jews who ranked high in the party and feared for their fate and privileges. Grossman, thinking blindly that the deaths of a few

---

1   +Doctor was a euphemism for Jew.

2   +Boris Yefimov (1900 - 2008), cartoonist.

might save a people threatened as a whole, put his signature to the letter together with the majority of those present. Perhaps Grossman's decision was provoked by his conversation at *Novy Mir*.

Grossman's home in Begovaya Street wasn't far from *Pravda*, so he walked home after he signed the letter with a heavy heart. He drank a hundred and fifty grams of vodka bought from one of the women vendors who were so common in the streets then, huddled in dirty overalls over their sheepskins.

Grossman reproached himself until the day he died for signing that letter. In *Life and Fate*, his character Shtrum, the physicist, finds himself acting similarly with the same bitter regrets.

Grossman loved Tvardovsky as a man and as a poet, so it mattered to him how Tvardovsky acted and spoke. Their argument blighted the history of *Life and Fate*. It could have been avoided. Their problems started in 1948, and though there was a reconciliation of sorts based on mutual respect and commitment to one another, their friendship was never reconstituted. Grossman's sense that Tvardovsky had behaved badly exacerbated rather than diminished with time. In September 1956, Grossman wrote to me in Dushanbe:

> I'll tell you what's been going on while you've been away. I've been to The Writers' Union and filed a petition with Azhayev[1] saying the Union needed to set up a commission to inquire into the possibility of rehabilitating dead writers who don't have families to initiate the process. I named Abram Lezhnev, Pilnyak, Andrei Novikov, and Svyatopolk-Mirsky. My proposal was met sympathetically. Azhayev promised to take the matter up with the Secretariat. I've had a chance to read the Presidium's report from

---

1   *Azhayev Vasily (1915-1968), Soviet writer, secretary of the USSR Writers' Union.

their archive. Tvardovsky's speech hurt me the most. After years it still embarrassed me to read it. I didn't think he could speak like that. He's cleverer than the others, and this enables him to be crueler. He's petty, although he's intelligent and talented.

I met with Simonov (whose speech I'd also read in the same archive, incidentally) at the Union. He was insistent and enthusiastic that I publish a second book at *Novy Mir*.

Oddly, Krivitsky phoned my house with the same proposal while I was with Simonov. He said to Olga Mikhailovna, 'I'm glad that I got you on the phone, knowing how complicated Vasily Semyonovich is. I thought he'd brush me off.'

He said, to Olga Mikhailovna, 'If Grossman keeps quiet, we'll speak to him in another language; let him know that we'll take a different approach.' So I thought that he was speaking to me in another language when he offered to print a second book of mine.

To contextualize this letter, Simonov and Tvardovsky crowned themselves at Novy Mir, alternately, like ancient Iranian shahs. In September 1956, it was Simonov who was the editor with Krivitisky as his deputy when they asked for *Life and Fate* without knowing its content.

Another language was spoken to Grossman after 5th March 1953 when Stalin died. We heard the news at Ilyinskoye, where we had neither radio nor newspapers, so we were isolated from events until one March morning when our neighbor Marusya, who sometimes helped us with housekeeping, said, "Did you hear? Stalin's not well." We didn't believe it; her message seemed fabulously beautiful, too joyful. We couldn't keep calm, we were so excited, so we decided to go to the station to find news.

We walked three kilometers in the solitude of that fresh snowy March evening, incredulous but hopeful. The newspaper stand was closed but next to the commuter train schedule hung a newspaper that said Stalin was ill. We stayed up all night talking, wondering if he'd die; of course he would; otherwise the newspaper wouldn't have said he was sick. Perhaps he was dead already. What would be next? Would it be better or worse? Eventually, things did get better; the doctor-murderers' case was dismissed, and Beria was executed.

Turning from major national events to literary affairs, the Second Congress of Writers was convened a year after Stalin's death and for the first time in twenty years. Grossman and I were delegates. Fadeyev mustered the courage to apologize to Grossman when he spoke publically, despite the presence of foreign guests. He said he'd been unfair in attacking *For A Just Cause* and its author. Both this, Fadeyev's last speech, and his subsequent suicide were expressions of good in a man doomed to be cruel. His suicide wasn't a sin before God but a manifestation of a desire to atone for sin by death. He had true, if moderate, talent. If he'd lived during the reign of the Tsar, he'd have been a minor writer, nothing else.

Today's dull, sterile-faced leaders of the Writers' Union don't care at all about the fate of Russian literature. Their heads don't ache for it, and they don't worry about the brightest talents who drain away from it: on the contrary, that makes their quiet and comfortable lives even easier. They don't care a straw that a book unpublished in Russia becomes a successful book abroad. They are more concerned about potential competitors at home. There may be no blood on their hands, they may not directly persecute anyone, largely as a result of external circumstances, but I think that had they been in Fadeyev's place in Moscow in the years of the Yezhov terror or the struggle with "rootless cosmopolitanism" they would have surpassed him in cruelty.

To return to the events of 1954, *For A Just Cause*, which had so recently been considered politically harmful, was now to be launched by Voengiz. Grossman had written to me in Dushanbe on 22nd July 1954:

Hello, dear friend!

I finally got your letter. Although it didn't walk but flew for seven days. While you've been away, a lot's changed in my life. A telegram from Fadeyev arrived in Zagoryanka saying 'For A Just Cause has been submitted for print without dissent by the Secretariat.[1] The matter is resolved positively and definitively. I shake your hand.' This was so unexpected that, at first, I thought it was a hoax. But back in Moscow, I found a letter from Colonel Krutikov[2]: 'Vasily Semyonovich, everything's alright; Surkov called and said it will be our great achievement if your book's approved by the Writers' Union. The leading authorities have already been consulted, so you don't need to send it to them.'

On the evening I got back from the country, Fadeyev called me to Moscow on some minor detail (he'd apparently decided to surpass the Gospel miracle and take part both in Lazarus' burial and rising). At a meeting in connection with the forthcoming Writers' Congress, where both A As[3] were present, it became clear that there were no reasons for delaying the book's publication or for further discussion of it with the Union.

So here's a summary of the facts. The book's already been signed off for print, and Krutikov brought me the cover design together with a second contract relating to mass publication [second edition]. The first edition is scheduled for this September and October.

---

1   +The area near Moscow where the Grossmans had rented a cottage. Grossman gave up his villa in Lianozovo to the homeless people who had settled there during the war.

2   *Colonel Krutikov, writer and editor of Voengiz Publishing House.

3   *Alexei Alexandrovich Fadeyev and Alexander Alexandrovich Surkov.

And I've had an unexpected letter from General Shcherbakov[1] saying that Voengiz intends to issue a further mass edition [third edition] of the novel in 1955. My dear, I'm sure you can well imagine the sensation I experienced. But of course, you have no idea how sad I was that you weren't in Moscow, that I couldn't share my thoughts and feelings with you. The book's had a long and arduous path, but your friendship's helped me through it. You've shared its path with me like a brother. But I don't think that it's ended, that we're in the Park of Culture and Rest. And I'm glad it's not over. If its progress is destined to be hard, let it be, but let it continue.

I remember Ilyinskoye, our summer idyll, the stove, playing durak, eating macaroni soup, walking to the station, and then thawing out. Manya rattling buckets. 'You remember so much ... listening to the relentless murmur of wheels.'

Syoma, when do you intend to return to Moscow? You've been away too long. Please write exactly when you plan to. I read your letter, and suddenly I wanted very much to visit this distant land I've never been to and walk through the wonderful garden you describe so poetically.

It was upsetting to read about the death of Ayni. What you write about his last days is so sad. I can feel that he was a good man.

You're asking about Moscow's news. I wasn't at Fadeyev's speech, but I heard it was brief. He asked not to have to report to the congress at length. His request was respected; Surkov just made Fadeyev introduce [The Second Writers' Congress] in a brief speech.

---

1   *Alexander Shcherbakov (1901-1945), Editor in Chief of the Voengiz publishing house.

As Grossman predicted, his thorny path hadn't ended. However, Grossman's thoughts and work continued, despite his sorrows and bitter joys: *Life and Fate* was being written.

When I asked what the second book's title would be, Grossman said, "In keeping with Russian tradition, it will consist of two words separated by the conjunction – and."

Years of daily labor passed as Grossman read me chapters and scenes from the novel. I saw Grossman's force of expression in them, which was already familiar to me, but I also found something new. He had become preoccupied with the theme of God, the theme of religion. It was no coincidence that the Catholic priest, Hardy, appeared in a German concentration camp, together with the miserable, Russian, failed God-seeker, Ikonnikov, who doesn't believe in good but believes in kindness. I couldn't agree with the observation given to Ikonnikov that "God is powerless to reduce life's evils," but I was struck by his thought that "piecemeal kindness constitutes what's human in man, is the human spirit's greatest achievement."

Major Yershov became especially dear to me. Prisoners in the German concentration camp "felt Yershov emanated a cheerful glow. His simple warmth, which everyone needed, came from the Russian oven."

The son of a dispossessed father, the Major becomes the leader of the imprisoned Soviet war commanders. And then come words that explain much about the mood and beliefs of the author:

> The Vlasov[1] proclamation said exactly what [Yershov's] father had said. [Yershov] knew its truth. But he knew that a truth, coming from the lips of the Germans and Vlasov, was a lie ... It was clear that in fighting against the Germans, he was fighting for a free Russian life. Victory would be a victory over Hitler and also over the death camps that killed his

---

1   +Andrei Andreievich Vlasov (1901-1946), Red Army general who collaborated with Nazi Germany during World War II.

mother, sister, and father.

And we see the Soviet camps. During those deadly, horrible years for our motherland, Grossman persistently questioned people, from near and far, who had miraculously survived and been freed from the camps. He collected and recorded a considerable body of evidence and became the first person to paint a broad picture of Russia dying behind barbed wire. *A Day In The Life of Ivan Denisovich*[1] hadn't been written for readers yet, but listening to Grossman, I learned for the first time things I had always suspected; that had always hurt and bled inside me. I learned them not as separate stories but in all their insane and maddening universality, and the minutiae and exactitude of their expression stunned me.

There is a view that since Grossman himself wasn't in a camp, what he wrote was hearsay. This isn't a literary view – Derzhavin[2] actively participated in the pursuit of Pugachev[3], but he didn't portray the peasant leader. This was done by Pushkin, who lived in a different century.[4] Both Pugachev's sheepskin, and the Kalmyk story that Pugachev told Grinev, are alive for us from childhood. It shouldn't be necessary to restate that artistic talent, emotional tension, and the researcher's integrity can combine to create the miracle of vivification.

In the German camp, something moves in the seemingly hardened consciousness of the old Bolshevik, Mostovsky: "Many things in his own soul were now foreign to him ..." and yet they sit tight in him. He favors the brutal Communist camp inmates' solution of denouncing the 'wonderful guy,' Yershov, which leads to his deportation to lethal Buchenwald because Yershov is "non-Party, extraneous, obscure."

1   +The first Soviet work on the Stalinist camps by Alexander Solzhenitsyn, 1962.
2   +Gavrila Romanovich Derzhavin (1743-1816), Russian statesman and one of its greatest poets before Alexander Pushkin.
3   +1773-1774 after the Pugachev's Rebellion.
4   +In *The Captain's Daughter* (1836), a novel giving a romanticized account of Pugachev's Rebellion.

But Mostovsky is killed in the camp too, and Magar, another old Bolshevik, dies there, albeit in a different manner; he hangs himself. Before he dies, he says to his fellow convict and former pupil:

'We didn't understand freedom; we crushed it. Even Marx didn't value it ... on the other side of the barbed wire, self-preservation tells people to change unless they want to die or be sent to a camp. And so Communists have created idols, put on uniforms and epaulets, started to preach nationalism, and attacked the working class. If necessary, they'll revive the Black Hundreds ... '

In the novel *For A Just Cause*, high-principled Bolsheviks Mostovsky and Krymov think and talk about Marx quite differently, as does Grossman.

After reading *Life and Fate*, one clever writer said to me: "What bad luck for Grossman – if only his novel, with its precise and stunning descriptions of the camps, had been published before Solzhenitsyn's."

I disagree. Of course, it would have been better if those who had somehow preserved the novel's manuscript had found the courage to care about its fate sooner. But I am firmly convinced that literary discoveries are not limited by their subjects.

Discovery in literature is always about characters. Each in his own way, Solzhenitsyn and Grossman discovered men in concentration camps. As for the topic, it's global, and no contemporary Russian writer has the right to ignore it. After all, the Camp and the Prison have powerfully and ominously entered the homes of almost every Soviet man, be it the metropolitan apartment, Ukrainian hut, or tent in the kishlak[1]. It inhabited virtually every family of – to use the old word – Philistines. It's said jokingly that the essence

---

1   +Kishlak is a rural settlement of semi-nomadic Turkic peoples of Central Asia and Azerbaijan.

of nineteenth-century Russian literature can be defined by the titles of two literary works, *Who is to Blame?*[1], and *What Should be Done?*[2] However, the essence of this century's Russian literature, the century of prisons, hospitals, and wars, can be identified by the titles, *The Gulag Archipelago, Cancer Ward*, and *Life and Fate*.

I learned a lot in Grossman's chapters about war in Stalingrad. I saw only what I was supposed to: our ships, armored motorboats, observation points on the right bank of the Volga, Rodimtsev's headquarters in the 'Drainpipe', Gorokhov's fortification on 'the Marketplace.' But Grossman described things the rank and file couldn't see or know about during the war. Grossman unfolded a panorama of one of its most significant battles, not only from a bird's eye helicopter view of all fronts, armies, corps, and divisions but also from below, with the eyes of a soldier in a trench. Before him, only Tolstoy had seen war with such double vision.

And there is a chapter about the famous 'Pavlov's House.'[3] Grossman calls this the 6/1 house. The 6/1 house is surrounded by the Germans, but its doomed inhabitants continue fighting and fighting hard. Grekov, their commander, was nicknamed 'the house manager.' The demise of this house is much more horrendous than that of Edgar Allan Poe's 'House of Usher' because everything in it is easier, both life and death. And in this hell shines the love of Sergei and Katya while Grekov's audacious character blazes. Now, the house is gone, Grekov is gone, but the reckless captain doesn't die in our souls; he still charms us with his Russian daring and moves with the poignant anguish of his sharp, brutal, and heartfelt Russian mind.

---

1   +1846 novel by Alexander Herzen.
2   +1863 novel by Nikolay Chernyshevsky.
3   +Pavlov's House was a fortified building during the Battle of Stalingrad (27th September–25th November 1942). It became known by that name because it was seized and defended by the platoon of Yaacov Pavlov during the battle.

The misadventures of Zhenya Shaposhnikova in Kuibyshev may seem dim compared to the horrors of the German and Soviet concentration camps, prisons, and gas chambers and the story of the 6/1 house. However, their impression has stayed with me since I heard Grossman reading the Kuibyshev pages. Strange to say, most writers guided by the formula 'being determines consciousness'[1] adore writing about consciousness and are highly unwilling to touch on being. Reading Balzac, Dickens, Tolstoy, and Dostoevsky, we always know what the tangible, everyday worries of the characters are, even how much money they have at a given time. In many of today's books, only the flawed characters are interested in money, and the good ones care either about industry and its processes or, in recent years, about their families. Before Grossman, almost no one had ever written about the quarrels and petty squabbles in the kitchens of communal apartments, about overcrowding in homes where elderly parents, daughters, their husbands, and grandchildren sleep in the same room together, so that as a Kuban peasant told me, "the hut sways to and fro." No one else wrote about long lines at the grocery stores, the meager salaries, stuffiness in the mornings on overcrowded buses and trams, an oxygen-less bureaucracy choking helpless people. We share the ordeals of Yevgenia Shaposhnikova, who cannot get a residence permit that would give her the right to live in the city. We find familiar tormentors in minor portraits such as those of the cowardly head of the design office where Shaposhnikova works and the unblinking, indifferent eyes of the passport office's chief in whose long hopeless queue Yevgenia stands. There she hears her fill of stories about those refused residence permits; daughters who had wanted to live with their mothers, a paralyzed woman who had wanted to live with her brother, another woman who had come to Kuibyshev to look after a war-invalid.

---

1   +Karl Marx, 'Preface' in *Contribution to the Critique of Politicial Economy* (Progress Moscow 1859).

When Grossman read me a letter from Shtrum's mother, he took off his glasses to wipe away his tears. Grossman was scorched by the Jewish apocalypse of the twentieth century. Some readers of *Life and Fate* said that the Nazi death camps for Jews and the fierce struggle against 'cosmopolitanism'[1] in our country changed Grossman as a person and a writer. I think people who hold this opinion have some grounds, but they forget that Grossman, above all, was a Russian writer. The beauty of Russian nature, its heart, unbearable suffering, purity and patience were the closest and most important issues to Grossman. It was no accident that in a letter from a Jewish mother from behind the barbed wire of the ghetto, these words appeared:

> Just like peasants looted Kulaks, their own neighbors robbed Jews.

These words are from the last letter Grossman's mother, Ekaterina Savelyevna, sent to him. *Life and Fate* is dedicated to her memory. Ekaterina Savelyevna was tortured and murdered in the Berdichev ghetto. For many years after she died, Vasily Semyonovich continued writing her letters, shared his thoughts and worries with her, and reported on the progress of the novel. The letters are preserved by Grossman's stepson, Fyodor Guber.

Jewish tragedy was, for Grossman, part of the tragedy of Russian and Ukrainian peasants, part of the general tragedy of the victims of an era of total destruction. Is there in Ukrainian literature a book that recounts the all-embracing fate of the Ukraine's peasants during collectivization in the way Grossman's *Everything Flows* does? He wouldn't have been a true Russian writer if he hadn't sought the human in the person of any nation.

---

1   +'Cosmopolitan' is the term used to refer to the tendency among some Soviet intellectuals, particularly writers, to express views which were deemed 'pro-Western' or 'antipatriotic.' The term was frequently used in reference to Jewish intellectuals.

This quest took him from *For A Just Cause* to *Life and
Fate*. As he penetrated man's depths, he gradually freed
himself from his former, sometimes inaccurate notions and
steadily approached the divine truth, "the individual human
being's miracle," embodied in the character of Sofya Osipovna
Levinton as she reached the threshold of the gas chamber.
The spinster befriends the boy, David, in the cattle car. They
find each other in the gas chamber, and the little boy, with
a bird's body, dies before her; his body sags in her hands.
"I've become a mother," she thinks. It's her last thought. And
David's eyes before his death meet with the curious eyes of a
German soldier, Rose, who stares through the glass. Is Rose a
human being? After all, "a human being exists as a world, never
repeatable by anybody in time's infinity. And a human being
experiences the happiness of freedom and goodness only when
finding in others what he has found in himself."

Grossman, like his Shtrum, knew only a dozen words of
Yiddish. He was well-educated and read French books in the
original from his childhood (his mother taught French) and
could recite by heart whole pages of Daudet's *Letters from the
Mill*, Maupassant's *Life*, and De Musset's poems but was poorly
versed in Jewish history. Seeing my volumes of *The Jewish
Encyclopedia* in Russian, he asked without much interest, "Do
you find anything important for yourself in them?"

But he definitely could not, both as a Jew and, I repeat,
especially as the Russian writer he was, remain indifferent to
one of the most terrible human catastrophes of our century.
While on one of his trips to the front line, it was Grossman who
disclosed Treblinka (his essay 'Treblinka Hell' was a booklet
distributed at the Nuremberg Trials). It was he who first wrote
literature describing the gas chambers (chapters named 'Gas'
were published in one of our newspapers before the arrest of
Life and Fate). It was he who witnessed the persecution of Jews
in the country of victorious socialism. And it was he who was

one of the initiators and editors of *The Black Book*[1], about the total extermination of the Jews by the Nazis in the temporarily occupied territories of the Soviet Union, which was destroyed at home and published abroad.

He was tormented and insulted by the fact that writers who were Russian by birth were not wounded to the quick by this horror. He was ashamed of them before the living eyes of the great Russian writers, philosophers, and scientists. When Yevtushenko's poem 'Babi Yar'[2] appeared in print in the early sixties, Grossman said, "Finally, a Russian wrote that antisemitism exists in our country. The poem is so-so, but the act of its writing is another matter; it's fine, even brave."

I've mentioned my impressions of some chapters of *Life and Fate* when Grossman read them to me over many years in his quiet, slightly raspy voice. But when in the early winter of 1960, he came to Chernyakhovskaya Street with the entire thousand-page novel, I read every word and then began to read it again immediately. I realized with all my being, mind, and heart that God gave me the good fortune to be one of the first (after probably only the family members and, of course, the typist) to read this great, and I hope, immortal work.

It would be ill-advised to consider *Life and Fate* only from the point of view that the author had changed politically and philosophically since he'd written *For A Just Cause*. Indeed he had, but in addition, the dark sides of reality are often the source of light for the mind of the artist. *Life and Fate* is far superior to and much more important than *For A Just Cause*, but both novels belong to the same solid talent in the same way

---

1 +Vasily Grossman and Ilya Ehrenburg eds., *The Black Book*: aka *The Ruthless Murder of Jews by German-Fascist Invaders Throughout the Temporarily-Occupied Regions of the Soviet Union and in the Death Camps of Poland during the War 1941-1945* (1946).

2 +1961 poem denouncing the Soviet distortion of the facts surrounding the massacre of Jews in the Ravine of Babi Yar, in Kiev, Ukraine (September 1941) in addition to the widespread anti-semitism still experienced in the Soviet Union.

that *Russian and Lyudmila* and *Boris Godunov* both belong to Pushkin and *Verses about the Beautiful Lady* and *The Twelve* belong to Blok.

After Pushkin wrote *Boris Godunov*, he exclaimed, "Well done, Pushkin, you son of a bitch!" After Blok finished *The Twelve*, he wrote in his diary, "Today I'm a genius." Grossman could have said something like that about himself when he wrote *Life and Fate*. But sadly, Grossman's thoughts as he finished his masterpiece were far from happy. He wrote to me on October 24, 1959, from the seaside village near Koktebel:

> I enjoy walks along deserted beaches so much. I really would like you to be here. You feel the sea so strongly here; it's not like Yalta; it's something special, wide, deserted. It's for dreamers, people with a future, and those with nothing to dream about except the past. And, of course, it's for poets. Both the excitement of youth and the sadness of spent life is audible to poets, so I want you to come here and wander for a few days to embrace the unembraceable.
>
> I've worked hard here and finished the third part. Corrected, cut, added (but mostly cut). I've taken time to say goodbye to people I was tied to every day for sixteen years. It's strange; we became so used to each other, at least I did.
>
> I'll come to Moscow soon and read the entire manuscript from start to finish for the first time. And although we understand that you reap what you sow, I keep wondering what I'll read there and how many readers it will have apart from the reader-writer. I think this fate can't be escaped. We'll see what's been sown.
>
> I'm not feeling joy, enthusiasm, or agitation, but some anxiety and worry, which, although vague, is very serious. Am I correct? That's the first and most

important question. Am I correct in front of the people and, therefore, in front of God?

And then the second question, did I cope as a writer? And then the third, the book's fate, its path? These days I've got a powerful feeling that the fate of the book is being separated from me. It will implement itself apart from me, removed from me when I am probably not here anymore. What was connected to me – couldn't have been without me – does it end now?

As our newspapers say, these things are the thoughts of Rubbish, the locksmith. Apart from my thoughts, there's my everyday life. Rubbish, the locksmith, eats, goes to the grocery store, and drinks beer. For some reason, Feodosiya this year is littered with mackerel. I eat mackerel and wash it down with turbid, young, white wine. This turbid costs 7 rubles and 50 kopecks a liter. Sometimes I eat mullet. I walk a lot, and you're right, I've really lost weight and gone brown in the sun. I'm as thin as a poplar, but I don't look too young. In the evening, Olga Mikhaylovna and I play 'A Thousand'[1].

My dear, don't write to me here, letters arrive so slowly, and I fear our letters will cross each other. If the sanatorium's agent doesn't fail with the tickets, we'll be in Moscow on the evening of November 5th. And if you find yourself at home, then we'll talk on the phone and agree to a meeting at The Founder[2].

I've coined an aphorism, "If the little bird sings too soon, her eggs will be snatched from the nest."[3]

---

1   +A card game, especially popular in Eastern Europe.
2   * Gorky's (founder of Soviet literature) monument in front of the Belarus railway station.
3   +From a Russian proverb "Рано птичечка запела, как бы кошечка не съела" – "If the little bird starts singing too early, the cat can eat it up," i.e. Don't get excited about success too soon - you don't know how things will turn out.

This really isn't an idea but a generalization …
Waiting to see you.
Love, Vasya.

As I re-read these lines, my heart shrinks. What prophetic sadness in a letter written at a time when the artist should have been engulfed by the great joy of victory. How distinct his vision was:

> … the fate of the book is being separated from me. It will implement itself apart from me, removed from me when I am probably not here anymore.

All this happened; true poets are always prophets. The day I read this letter, I hadn't anticipated, couldn't have foreseen what would happen. I just noted happily that my friend, for the first time, wrote the word "God" as I thought it should be written, with a capital letter. This passage appears in the same letter:

> I read Faulkner's stories. Most of them were published in *Inostrannaya Literatura*[1]. He's a strong, talented writer, a bit mannered, but to serious purpose. He thinks about life, doesn't use literary devices for their own sake, and his depiction is excellent, vivid, and concise. This is a talent.

Grossman's thoughts on the manner of writing gave me the opportunity to note here that in art, nothing becomes obsolete as quickly as technique. Only the characters live on without growing old. Of course, we remember and repeat with delight the metaphors, tropes, and witty, thoughtful expressions in our favorite books, both Russian and translated. Who can forget Hamsun's phrase: "Love isn't glycerin, it's nitroglycerin," or

---

1 +*Inostrannaya literatura* [*Foreign Literature*] a monthly literary magazine, publishing the best novels, stories and factual prose of foreign authors in Russian translation.

Cervantes' report that Sancho Panza stepped into the bushes to do what "no one else could do for him." However, all these brilliant phrases only make sense when they are working to create eternal characters, such as Don Quixote, Sancho Panza, and Prince Myshkin. If a writer's characters don't endure, then the writer doesn't.

Once I'd read *Life and Fate* as a whole, I knew that the thoughts of flesh and blood had, as Dostoevsky's Versilov said, "entered words," and at least two of its characters, Getmanov and Grekov, would endure among literature's most significant. All the characters in the novel are well achieved; they live with us, Red Army soldiers and generals, the young, the old, peasants, academics, Germans, Russians, Armenians, Tatars, convicts, investigators, camp inmates, their jailors, beauties, plain Janes and more. I'd like to focus on one, Beryozkin, already memorable from *For A Just Cause.*

The middle-aged Major, who wears a repeatedly washed but neat army blouse, has bravely and cleverly fought in the forests of western Belorussia since the summer of 1941. He's gone through all the trials of war without being decorated or noticed by the high command. At Stalingrad, Aristov, who's been Beryozkin's subordinate, but is now a successful military business executive, sees his faded blouse and tarpaulin boots and thinks, "Well, if I'd fought a fraction as much as you have, how I'd have climbed the ranks by now."

And the old woman, in whose house Aristov was billeted, says to Major Beryozkin in Aristßov's absence:

> I can see by looking at you what kind of man you are, Major; you feel honest, the sort of man the State's based on, loyal. But this friend of yours, Aristov, what kind of soldier's he? Can someone like that really understand things? To him, the State's based on alcohol.[1]

---

1   +This episode and the character of Aristov are absent in the published version of *Life and Fate.*

At this crucial point, the State begins to understand who it's based on, the battalion commander Filyashkin, the non-Party Colonel Novikov, the physicist Shtrum, downtrodden by the people of the Science Department, the brave, myopic writer Grossman. It's only Captain Grekov that the State doesn't understand, and, in its own way, the State is right.

Major Beryozkin is promoted at Stalingrad and entrusted to command the regiment where Grekov's 6/1 house is situated. On the eve of the decisive battle, Beryozkin falls seriously ill. "He was lying in his bunker; his face was burning, and his eyes looked transparent and vacuous."

He seems not to hear a thing going on in the bunker. A letter from his wife arrives, the first in a long time. One of the commanders begins to read it to him, "Hello, my Vanya, hello, my dearest, hello, my beloved …." Beryozkin comes to life, turns his head, and says, "Give it to me." And, after reading the letter, he says, "You must get me back in shape today." Beryozkin washes in a petrol drum, half filled "with steaming-hot river water."

That night Beryozkin recovers, and General Chuikov calls him:

> "You do sound a bit hoarse," Chuikov almost gloats. "Well, the Germans will give you some hot milk. They've got it ready, and they won't be long."
>
> "Yes, comrade," says Beryozkin, "I understand."
>
> "Very good," says Chuykov. "But if you ever think of retreating, remember I can make you an egg flip at least as good as the Germans' hot milk."

The battle takes place in the Tractor Plant's shops. Beryozkin's regiment withstands the enemy's pressure. Again a phone rings and Chuikov's tense and quiet voice is heard on the receiver:

> "Beryozkin? The Divisional Commander's wounded.

His Second-in-Command and Chief of Staff are dead. I order you to take command yourself." Then, more slowly and with emphasis, "You held their attack. You commanded the regiment through hellish, unheard-of conditions. Thank you, my friend. I embrace you."

Beryozkin is written so well, despite the fact he isn't a new character, he is a contemporary version of Tolstoy's Captain Tushin[1]. But nobody, prior to Grossman, not even Tolstoy, had portrayed characters like Getmanov and Grekov, for to do this you had to understand the depths of men nurtured on our Soviet reality.

Dementy Trifonovich Getmanov, the Secretary of the Obkom[2], of an area of the Ukraine now occupied by Germans, had been made Commissar of a tank corps being assembled in the Urals. Before he left for the corps, Getmanov boarded a Douglas Dakota to Ufa, where his family had been evacuated.

These quiet words begin Getmanov's story. Grossman had tried to draw a regional committee secretary in the novel *For A Just Cause*, but as a type, Pryakhin was unsuccessful; a journey into this man's heart didn't take place. Lacking the critic's talent, I find it difficult to outline Getmanov's colossal character. I'm tempted to facilitate the task by writing down everything Grossman said about Getmanov, a peasant's son. It can't really be effectively paraphrased, extraordinary as that may seem:

He hadn't fought in the Civil War, been hunted by the police, or been exiled to Siberia by a Tsarist court order. ... In his youth, Getmanov was bright and

---

1   +*War and Peace*, Leo Tolstoy (1869).
2   +Obkom - the Party committee of an oblast or province.

obedient, ... he'd been called to do security work and soon became the bodyguard of the Obkom, the oblast Party committee. 'An Oblast', in common parlance, loyal to the Party ... The sacrifices Getmanov made in the name of Party loyalty were cruel sometimes. His was a world where neighbors from your village or teachers you've been indebted to since childhood no longer existed; neither love nor sympathy figured anymore. Words like 'shunned'; 'didn't help'; 'destroyed', 'betrayed' no longer operated ... Loyalty showed itself when there wasn't even a need for sacrifice when personal feelings didn't survive even for a moment if they happened to clash with the spirit of the Party ...

The power of a Party leader does not require the scientist's talent or writer's gift. It is something superior to either. Getmanov's directives were anxiously awaited by hundreds of singers, writers, and scientific researchers. Getmanov couldn't sing, play the piano, direct a play, or really understand science, poetry, music, or painting, but what he said could determine what happened to the Head of Department at a university, an engineer, a bank manager, Trade Union Chairman, Kolkhoz or theatrical production.

Grossman observes keenly that Getmanov, going to the front, is interested not in the enemy but his corps commander Novikov, a man without 'nomenclature'[1], an enigma, a protégé of war. Getmanov is extremely concerned not about the formation of the corps but that (as he's previously discovered) Novikov is going to marry Krymov's ex-wife, the same Krymov that's had numerous, long-standing ties with both the right

---

1   +The Nomenklatura was the register kept by the party organs of people eligible for posts of responsibility.

wing and the Trotskyists. Getmanov later destroys Krymov at the front.

Before Getmanov leaves, he gives a farewell party attended by his brother-in-law Sagaydak (a senior official of the Ukrainian Central Committee) and former newspaper editor.

In his role as editor, Sagaydak might consider it appropriate to pass over some event: a bad harvest, an ideologically inconsistent poem, a formalist painting, an outbreak of foot-and-mouth disease, an earthquake, or the destruction of a battleship. He might prefer to close his eyes to a terrible fire in a mine or a tidal wave that swept thousands of people from the face of the earth. In his view, these events had no meaning ... He felt that his power, skill, and experience as an editor were revealed by his ability to bring to the consciousness of his readers only those ideas that were necessary and of true educational benefit. Getmanov's friend Mashuk (a security officer) also attends the farewell party and something unpleasant happens. As Mashuk leafs through a photograph album he finds a portrait of Stalin:

> ... his face scrawled over in coloured pencil, a blue pointed beard added to his chin and light-blue earrings hanging from his ears.

Although only Getmanov's intimates were at the party, he and his wife were particularly unnerved. They were of course afraid of Mashuk. "It's just a child's prank,"said Sagaydak. 'It's not just a prank, it's malicious hooliganism,' said Getmanov with an angry sigh."

It wouldn't be worth speaking about Getmanov if he were written two-dimensionally. But he isn't. He's clever, a good judge of character, understands the state machine, and knows how to talk to a Red Army private and charm him with his direct, familiar manner. While he's never been at the front, the military says of him, "Our Commissar's suave, isn't he."

Although there had previously been fictional characters who had something in common with Getmanov, Grossman is unique in fleshing out the type. The way Getmanov emotes comes as a shock. Although he has a mistress while he serves in the corps, he still feels angry when Commander Belov, a married man, finds himself falling in love with a nurse. Grekov says to Belov, "... don't let your personal life disgrace you."

Getmanov's capable of magnanimity. He seconds the toast Novikov makes to Stalin, even though it comes at the wrong time, saying, "Yes, let's drink to the old man, our Father, under whose leadership we've marched on the Volga."

Getmanov can joke, "Fritz's done more to put the peasants' back up in one year than we Communists have in twenty five." But Grossman says of Getmanov's tendency to speak out, "far from being infectious [it] tended to unnerve the man he addressed."

Getmanov's feelings are chilling, and he considers betrayal to be noble in circumstances he thinks necessary. After Novikov delays the final (successful) offensive by eight minutes, contravening both the Commander at the front and at the top, he and the Corps Command celebrate victory and are congratulated by Stalin. "Thank you, Pyotr Pavlovich!" says Getmanov to Novikov, "A Russian thank you, a Soviet thank you, a Communist thank you, I raise my hat."

Getmanov is feeling sincere, and with the same sincerity, he writes a denunciation to the senior authorities saying that the Corps' Commander arbitrarily delayed commencement of the decisive battle for eight minutes in violation of Stalin's order.

That's Getmanov; a tirelessly active, short man with a large head, matted hair, broad shoulders, a big belly, and tiny, clever, penetrating eyes. This is how we remember him and how he'll be remembered by those who read *Life and Fate* after we're gone.

Pavlov's house has been the subject of countless poems and a great deal of prose. It's a place of pilgrimage for visitors to Stalingrad (Volgograd) who want to commemorate our soldiers' bravery. Grossman was the only correspondent who saw it surrounded by German soldiers, but his pen drew not only what he saw at the house of the condemned but also what was happening in the country where he was born.

I once asked Grossman if *Life and Fate*'s Grekov was a fictionalized version of Yakov Pavlov. He answered, "Grekov has elements of Chekov." In this instance, Chekov is the sniper in Grossman's catchily entitled essay 'Through Chekov's Eyes' (in 1946, Ehrenberg entitled his review of Grossman's war stories, 'Things Seen Through Grossman's Eyes').

The two double-syllable names he uses are both based on the names of nations. And Grekov, the novel's hero, conforms to a national stereotype.

When the house's wireless connection breaks and the regiment's Commissar tires of the strictures of command as the house faces demise, he is still alarmed that Grekov has got entirely out of hand and spoken heresy to the men, despite his fighting courageously against the Germans. What was Grekhov's heresy? Statements like:

> "No one's got the right to lead other people like sheep. Even Lenin never understood that. A revolution is supposed to free people. But Lenin said: 'In the past, you were badly led. I'm going to lead you well.'"

I, too, heard similar views articulated when I was in the dugouts. Fear of authority recedes as death approaches, as you feel it breathing on you. The soldiers in the 6/1 house weren't simpletons. Young Seryozha is surprised at what he sees as the courage with which they criticize the Ministry of Interior, the pain and abandon with which they describe the grief and suffering which afflicted the poor peasantry during the Collectivization Campaign. These same soldier peasant-critics fight desperately for the last tiny piece of their homeland, this house located on the axis of the enemy's attack.

When the famous mystery of the Russian soul is unraveled, it's simply the human soul. During a German air raid, the

short-sighted Lieutenant Batrakov, who taught maths before
the war, sits calmly reading a book above the bombed stair-
case in the ill-fitting glasses he's taken from a dead German.
Grekov utters a wonderful, purely Russian phrase: "... no
shit German will triumph here. Who could against this kind
of fool?" Grekov sees Batrakov and Ivanushka as generous,
warm, unselfish fools, the type depicted in *Russian Fairy Tales*,
who wouldn't leave the 6/1 house even though they knew
they would all die there. In fact, unbidden by his superiors,
Seryozha returns to 'Grekov's house' from the staff bunker, and
Grekov says, "He did well. [He] wouldn't have rejoined us until
the next world otherwise."

Soshkin, a political officer, says of his visit to the 6/1 house:

> "The men all seem terrified of this Grekov, but he
> just acts like one of them. They all go to sleep piled
> up together on the floor, Grekov included, and they
> call him Vanya. I'm sorry to say, but it seems more
> like a sort of Paris Commune than a military unit."

Based on Soshkin's report, a case is opened against Grekov
at the very high echelon of the Front's Political Department. If
only that department had known how the 6/1 house's doomed
talked about Katya, the radio operator, that Oshkin had
brought them:

> "All I care about are a woman's breasts."
> "Even a Katya looks good here. In the land of the
> blind, the one-eyed man is a king. She's got legs of
> a stork, no bottom to speak of, and giant cow eyes."
> "You just like big breasts; you're old school,
> pre-revolutionary."
> "Who'll get her in the end?"
> "It's obvious – Grekov."

The Privates aren't allowed to speak about their
Commanders like that. But Grekov does want to grab Katya

and feel her warmth while he dictates reports to regimental headquarters. He reigns supreme in the 6/1 House; he's strong-willed and cruel at times. He tells Seryozha to go to regimental headquarters, which would mean leaving Katya, whom he loves and who loves him back. As Grekhov gives Seryozha a chance at life, Seryozha thinks:

> "We're being expelled from Paradise. He's separating us like two serfs."

The narrative continues:

> [Seryozha] gave Grekov a look of mingled hatred and entreaty ... [feeling] there was something quite horrible about Grekov's look, something insolent and merciless ...

But Grekov suddenly says:

> "And the radio operator can go with you. You can show her the way to Headquarters." Seryozha suddenly understood that he'd never seen such sad, intelligent, wonderful eyes in his life."

Grekov is the lovers' savior, and the new Daphnis and Chloe, war's children, escape death in the 6/1 House. Before the war, infantry captain Grekov read books, went to the movies, played cards with a friend, drank vodka, and quarreled with his jealous wife. During the war, he fascinates both rank and file and commanders and evokes admiration with his amazing mix of strength, courage, and the ability to rise above life's routines. Headquarters order him to give a detailed report on the radio every day at nineteen hundred hours, but Grekov knocks the radio operator's hand off the switch and says with a grin:

> "A fragment from a mortar bomb has put the wireless set out of action. Contact will be re-established when it suits Grekov."

In the 6/1 House, "watched by the whole world," Grossman steers Grekov into a collision course with the conventional Krymov, who, at mortal risk, sneaks into the house to make the case against Grekov:

"[Who] provoked and defied in every respect, by a glance, movement, the set of his wide, flat nostrils. "Never mind," Krymov thought, "I'll bend you."

But he doesn't bend Grekov. This high-ranking Comintern worker, who'd known Trotsky, Bukharin, and prominent figures of the international Communist movement, this courageous participant of the Civil and Patriotic Wars, armed with all his Marxist-Leninist theory, is powerless in the face of this infantry captain with his people's truth. In addition, Krymov fails in his communications with the fighters, and their sense of imminent death weakens their relationship with the Commissar:

A sapper, whose head was bound in a dirty, bloodstained bandage, asks Krymov, "And what about the kolkhozes, comrade? Couldn't we have them liquidated after the war?"

"Yes," said Grekov, "could we have a lecture on that?"

"I'm not here to lecture," said Krymov. "I'm a fighting Commissar. I've come here to stop certain unacceptable partisan attitudes that have taken root in this building."

"OK," said Grekov. "but who'll stop the Germans?"

"Don't worry, we'll find someone. And I'm not here, as it's been said, to drink a bowl of soup but to give you a taste of Bolshevism."

"Excellent," said Grekov, "I'm ready for it."

Krymov continued in a firm tone with only a hint of mockery, "And comrade Grekov, if need be, you'll be on the menu."

The honest, decent Krymov decides Grekov will be on the menu and denounces him in writing. However, the vile, worthless careerists eat Krymov instead. But this is our native madness, the heretic Grekov is lauded and dies heroically, and the obedient Krymov's destiny is a senseless agonizing death in a prison cell.

When I read *Life and Fate* in the winter of 1960 and thought about the people I'd met in the novel, an idea crossed my mind: these fellow Russians, Getmanov and Grekov, Krymov and the NKVD lieutenant colonel who beat him were all so estranged from each other. The slightest twist of fate could have made their lives different, brought them together, or made them close. No wonder:

> … the Officer trampling over him now wasn't someone alien to him. Krymov could see himself now, could recognize himself as a boy weeping with joy over the astonishing terms of the *Communist Manifesto*, 'Workers of the World, Unite!'
> And this sense of recognition devastated him.

Reading the book, I realized, although not immediately, that the relationship between life and fate is far more complicated than I had previously thought. It can't be understood rationally. Fate can't be changed, it's created by life, and life is God. Writers, philosophers, and politicians wonder in vain what might have happened to Russia if Tsar Nikolai had been cleverer or Kerensky more serious and proactive. This is all empty speculation. Russia went on the path given to her, and on this path, Beryozkin, Grekov, Shtrum, Yershov, Levinton, and Ikonnikov shone as torches of hope. I don't know whether the Kingdom of God on Earth is possible, but I do know that the Kingdom of God exists inside us. Therefore, we're stronger than evil, and Russia is stronger than evil.

While reading the novel, I also had some less profound but – how can I put it – simpler, more pleasing thoughts. In some characters, I joyously recognized aspects of people I'd known, when and under which circumstances they'd said a given phrase.

Rurikovich Shargorodsky is, of course, our mutual friend Prince Zvenigorodsky, who wrote poems marked by the lovely influence of Afanasy Fet[1]. Zvenigorodsky used to say to us in his old man's hoarse, deep voice, "Both the Soviet and anti-Soviet public recognize my poetry, and neither publishes it."

Grossman's daughter, Katya, accidentally overheard young men talking about her appearance when she was a girl. She told her father this with her characteristic humor. The Red Army privates in the 6/1 House use precisely the same terms overheard by Katya.

The Commissar of Rodimtsev Headquarters, located in the 'Drainpipe', says to Krymov:

> "I had to drive Pavel Fyodorovich Yudin, a Moscow lecturer, to the Front in my car. I was warned by a Military Council member who said, '... if he loses a single hair off his head, I'll blow yours off.'"

A chapter about Rodimtsev's 'Drainpipe' appeared in one of our newspapers. I remember Elena Usievich, Mikhail Lifshitz, and someone else sent Grossman a sharp letter; they'd imagined that Rodimstev's Commissar's character maligned their friend, the party philosopher-academician, Yudin, whom Grossman did, in fact, despise.

In Maria Ivanovna Sokolova, I easily recognized Ekaterina Zabolotskaya. Grossman walked out with Ekaterina in the same way Shtrum walked out with Sokolova in the Neskuchny garden. Other familiar details of their relationship appear. I don't want to write about Grossman's last love, which brought him happiness and suffering in considerable measure and caused misery for four good people. For me, it's still too early

---

1   +Afanasy Afanasyevich Fet (1820-1892), Russian poet.

and too painful to do so.

In Grossman's text, pilots in the bunker sing the song 'The plane is spinning in a tailspin.' I remember Tvardovsky singing this song in Moscow during the summer of 1943. His voice was weak but clear. Grossman often repeated the words of the song after that.

Tungusov, the old cavalier guard, spins a yarn for camp inmates in barracks, combining *Lawrence of Arabia*, *The Three Musketeers*, and *The Travels of Jules Verne in Nautilus*. Our friend Semyon Grigoryevich Gecht, imprisoned for eight years, did the same for his criminal cellmates. And if the listener found contradictions in the narrative, Gecht, like Tungusov in the novel, just smartly dodged his critics with, "Nadine's situation merely seemed hopeless."

One night, when Gecht was being interrogated, at a moment of exhaustion, he told his investigator that he'd been praised in the Soviet press. To which the investigator replied, "Did you come here to get a diploma?" We read these exact words said to Krymov by his investigator.

When we were still friends, Nikolai Chukovsky told me that his Uncle Chaim, who lived in Kharkiv, called himself Edward. His puzzled nephew asked him why and was given the explanation, "Don't you know that in England, all Chaims are called Edward?" In the novel, the accountant's name, Edward Isaakovich Buckman, similarly denotes his origins.

Grossman liked teasing his stepson Fyodor when he reached puberty by quoting Gogol: "Well, brother, you've come out in stars"; Shtrum teases his stepson Tolya in the same terms.

During the struggle with 'cosmopolitanism,' an article by the Politburo member's son Yuri Zhdanov was published in *Pravda*. The piece referred to Einstein's work as 'Einstein's Theory.' Grossman was furious. In the novel, a young man from the Department of Science similarly speaks of Einstein's theory as 'so-called,' and Shtrum reacts to it with the same indignation as Grossman did.

There are quite a few places like that in the novel. Additionally, I read sentences and pages which reflect my own work with particular emotion, such as my poems about how the Germans burnt a gypsy woman on the shores of the Volga, about the Kalmyk steppe, and my feeling of freedom while I wandered it. "Freedom ... Freedom," Lieutenant-Colonel Darensky repeats, driving along the Kalmyk steppe, and my poem is called 'Freedom.' (Joseph Brodsky, who later edited my first book for Ardis, named the whole book after this poem. I could not have named it better.)

One day while working on the novel, Grossman said to me, "Well, your detail's faultless. Remember my Darensky? I gave him your feelings about the steppe's freedom as a punishment to you for not publishing your work."

Speaking of Lieutenant Colonel Darensky, he also appears in *For A Just Cause*. Tvardovsky, who published the novel in his magazine, chided the author about this being another Jewish name, but it was Grossman's housekeeper's name, Natasha, and she was a gentile peasant.

Now I'll turn to the fateful events that led Grossman to give *Life and Fate* to the journal *Znamya* [*The Banner*] to publish. Above all, Grossman's sharp resentment against Tvardovsky motivated his decision. This was the most fatal and significant reason. It makes no sense to assume that *Novy Mir* would have published *Life and Fate*. However, I can assert with authority that the novel would not have been arrested if the manuscript had been in "*Novy Mir*'s hands." Tvardovsky would not have sent the manuscript to the authorities. But Grossman did not want to deal with the editor who had renounced him. It was the grudge not only of an author but also of a former friend.

Grossman was also possessed by the strange idea that our progressive writers and editors are more cowardly than the official reactionaries. The latter, he thought, had the power, vim, and audacity of bandits. They, unlike the progressives, were able to take risks on occasion.

This strange idea was reinforced by one event. Grossman gave his remarkable story 'Tiergarten' to the liberal anthology *Literaturnaya Moskva* [*Literary Moscow*]. 'Tiergarten' was later printed in *Nash Sovremennik* [*Our Contemporary*]. The editor of *Literaturnaya Moskva* was Emmanuel Kazakevich[1], whose intellect and talent Grossman appreciated. True, Grossman had been angry with Kazakevich, who, on his recommendation, had accepted an extensive collection of my poems for his almanac at a time when I hadn't been published as an original poet for nearly a quarter of a century. At the last minute, Kazakevich, deferring to higher authorities, rejected my work. Kazakevich tried to console me that the same fate had befallen Pasternak's poems.

Grossman had a serious talk with Kazakevich, after which he decided to take one of my poems. Although it was utterly harmless, it was nonetheless accompanied by an explanatory translation, just in case. Grossman was satisfied to a degree. Relations between him and Kazakevich seemed to improve, but they went wrong again when Grossman submitted 'Tiergarten.' Kazakevich hesitated to publish it in the anthology, although he intended to take Yashin's[2] story, 'Levers', that castigated some manifestations of bureaucracy evoking the duality of consciousness. Kazakevich, not without reason, saw in 'Tiergarten' a mirror that would encourage readers to think about the similarity between the Russian and German regimes. After Grossman's death, Atarov, in the preface to the book *Dobro Vam*, containing 'Tiergarten', praised the story with skill, calling it anti-Fascist. In September 1956, Grossman wrote to me in Dushanbe:

The whole thing with Kazakevich takes a monstrous

---

1   +Emmanuel Kazakevich (1913–1962), Soviet writer who published in both Yiddish and Russian.
2   +Alexander Yashin (1913–1971), Soviet writer of *Village Prose*.

turn. I finally called Nikitina[1] and said: "Tell Kazakevich to call me today." I'm enured to editorial boorishness, but this surpasses anything I've seen. I thought that he'd call me in an hour, but days have passed, and it's been absolute silence instead. What a fantastic boor. I've written him a letter, but I don't know whether it's worth trying to shoot a sparrow with a cannon. It would be good to have your advice now, Semushka[2]. This time your stay in Central Asia has felt very painful from its first day on.

In the end, the editorial board of the almanac headed by Kazakevich rejected 'Tiergarten.' One could understand them; they were trying to prove to the authorities that writers could produce a good anthology in good faith. However, the almanac was criticized by the Party and was soon forced out of existence. Grossman didn't want to understand its editors. He considered them cowards and believed that after Stalin's death, they should all have squeezed the slave out of themselves.[3]

Just at this point in time, when Grossman's nerves were so strained, the chief editor of *Znamya*, Vadim Kozhevnikov[4], asked Grossman to give the novel to his journal. Kozhevnikov, who may have been aware that Grossman didn't have a penny at this time, offered him a substantial advance for a work he hadn't seen. Grossman didn't agree at first. He tried to test Kozhevnikov by offering him 'Tiergarten.' The magazine took it, but when Kozhevnikov had it typeset, the censor forbade its publication, seeing an allusion to Soviet reality in this story about Germans. Kozhevnikov had been blameless; there was no

---

1   *Editorial Secretary of the almanac.

2   +A diminutive of Semyon.

3   +A reference to Anton Chekhov's words: "Write about this man who, drop by drop, squeezes the slave's blood out of himself until he wakes one day to find the blood of a real human being - not a slave's - coursing through his veins." (Anton Chekhov to A S Suvorin, January 7th 1889).

4   +Vadim Kozhevnikov (1909-1984), Siberian poet and official Soviet writer.

cunning on his part. He really wanted to print the story.

Grossman believed this or at least allowed Kozhevnikov to convince him this was the case. And he finally decided to entrust his novel's fate to *Znamya*. It's relevant, too, that Grossman had once been close to this journal. Some of his work had appeared in it, and its editor was interested in Grossman's novel because his first book, *For A Just Cause*, had been successful. The second would attract many readers, raising the journal's reputation, which had faded at that time when *Novy Mir* dominated.

In addition, the few excerpts of *Life and Fate* that had been published in various newspapers – one fragment, strange to say, in *Vechernyaya Moskva* [*Evening Moscow*] – caused quite a literary stir and were much talked about. Reading these fragments at the time, it was impossible to guess at the essence of the novel in its entirety. Krivitsky[1] played his part; he'd become an influential member of the editorial board of *Znamya* after Stalin's death. He realized that he and Simonov had made a mistake by refusing to publish *For A Just Cause* and wanted to be part of the novel's success if it materialized, although I could be wrong about that. Krivitsky was very tough, and during the war, he'd been Platonov's benefactor. Once, Grossman and I visited Platonov pursuant to a prior engagement. He approached us in his dark narrow corridor and whispered, "Brothers, Krivitsky's turned up so ..." He was interrupted by Krivitsky, who appeared and stammered, "Hello, I've come out to see you both so that Andrei Platonovich doesn't have the time to curse me to you."

On 30th July 1960, Grossman wrote to me:

> Moscow's incredible heat is stubborn. I endure it with difficulty. The problem is not only that despite all my concessions, *Trud* [*Labor*] didn't print the excerpt from the novel, but also that they were so deceitful

---

1   +Alexander Zinovy Krivitsky (1910-1986), writer and journalist.

and hypocritical that I felt sick. Meanwhile, *Znamya*'s editors are pressing me for the manuscript and asking what date I'll submit it.

From my memory, Grossman finally completed the work in 1960. Before carrying the manuscript to the journal's office, he asked me to reread the whole novel and answer two questions: 1) Do you think that after the inevitable cuts, inserts, and heavy and light injuries, there's still a real possibility that the novel will be published? and 2) Which places, in your opinion, can't even be shown to the editors and should be removed in advance?

So I read *Life and Fate* for the third time, and as often happens, I found a lot of beauty I hadn't noticed before and felt the power of artistic cognition of man in the world and the world in man. When I finished reading, I took a taxi and brought the two heavy folders to Begovaya.

I answered Grossman's first question like this: "There's no hope that the novel will be published."

I begged him not to give the novel to Kozhevnikov, whose personality was fairly well-known to all writers. An angry expression I knew well appeared on Grossman's face.

"Well," he said, "do you think that when they read the novel, I'll be sent to prison?"

"Possibly," I said.

"And the book, even castrated, can't be printed?" he asked.

"Impossible. Neither Kozhevnikov nor Tvardovsky will print it, but you can show it to Tvardovsky at least. He not only has talent but is also a decent man."

Grossman looked at me with anger; his lips trembled.

"I won't be a coward like you. I'm not going to hide my manuscripts in a drawer for a quarter of a century like you! While Platonov kicked against the pricks, while I was beaten and trampled on, you quietly indulged in luxury and comfort while translating your Eastern customers."[1]

I thought that Grossman was being unfair to me. I had tried to publish my own work under Stalin, but Grossman had said himself that these attempts were futile. On the other hand, I felt that he, in fact, was right. I didn't kick against the pricks. Grossman also made me question my ideas about our society, particularly those related to the value of developing the national consciousness of the Soviet Union's diverse nations and cultures. I did understand the seriousness of Grossman's moral force and experienced its influence. When I later took a decisive turn in my life, I imagined what Grossman would have said, and I thought I heard his endorsement of my act.

There was a heavy silence. Finally, Grossman, breathing asthmatically, asked, "Did you suggest cuts?" I began to read the note I'd prepared. I'd selected a few of the most dangerous parts, around fifteen to twenty of them, although, in fact, all of the novel was dangerous. Sometimes my notes extended to several pages, sometimes, a few lines. I think the proposed cuts totaled no more than one and a half or two author's units. I remember I suggested he throw out Liss and Mostovskoy's whole conversation, where the Gestapo says to the old Bolshevik:

> When we look into each other's faces, we look into the mirror – our victory is your victory.

I drew attention to a few of Grossman's lines, not in terms of their danger but on different grounds. Here are these lines:

> A poet, a peasant by birth, endowed with intelligence and talent, wrote a sincere poem that praised the bloody time of peasant's suffering, a time that devoured his honest and simple-minded hard-working father.

---

1   *The expression, "Praslin kicked against the pricks," stems from Sergeyev-Tsensky's story, 'Deryabin the Bailiff.'

Grossman agreed humbly and cut all the passages I'd selected. Among these were the lines which were obviously based on Tvardovsky. Once Tvardovsky received the manuscript, Grossman was glad he hadn't included them.

When the copy of the first edition of *Life and Fate* published abroad reached me, I found it contained both the lines about Tvardovsky and the conversation between Liss and Mostovskoy. From this, I confirmed that its publishers hadn't received *Znamya*'s copy of the manuscript but the full, unabridged one. The publisher explained that for technical reasons (the quality of the microfilms of the manuscript), the book had gaps of different sizes. If memory serves me correctly, these gaps were small.

Going back to our rendezvous and subsequent to my having read the completed manuscript, I'll focus on one detail, which explains something about Grossman's state of mind. At the end of the conversation, I said, "Vasya, your punctuation's completely awry. I've tried to sort it out, but you'll have to transfer the edits to your other copies."

Grossman flared up. "The novel was nothing except punctuation to you!"

But after he saw the astonishment in my eyes, he quickly hugged me with tears in his own.

Week after week, month after month passed, he heard nothing from *Znamya*. He didn't want to call the editor first, but preferred to wait. Viktor Nekrasov, who was in good odour at *Znamya*, promised Grossman he'd scout around and report back at a certain time on a given day. Olga Mikhailovna, hospitable beyond their means, prepared a good meal and drinks and I was invited to join their warm table with this talented writer whom I'd met briefly at Maleyevka's house. We awaited his arrival 'til late in the evening but he didn't come – he probably forgot and was out drinking. Grossman was cut to the quick as he loved Nekrasov, both as a writer and as a man.

A few more months went by with with no word from the

journal. Completely exhausted, Grossman had an idea. At that time, our old friend Nikolai Chukovsky's literary and bureaucratic career was burgeoning, and he'd become a member of the editorial board of *Znamya*. Although I was by then attending translators' conferences less frequently, having lost patience with them, when I did go, I'd see Chukovsky. Grossman asked me to make inquiries of him at the next translator event I attended. Kolya[1] answered my questions willingly, saying, "I haven't read Vasily Semionovich's novel. As far as I know, none of the board's non-party members have.

"It's said that Kozhevnikov, Krivitsky, and Skoryno[2] have hidden the novel from everyone. Last week we all went to a readers' conference in Leningrad. I was in Kozhevnikov's carriage on the train, and I asked him about *Life and Fate*.

"He just growled, 'Grossman's let us down,' and changed the subject."

The translators' meeting ended late, at eleven p.m. but knowing that Grossman was anxious and waiting for me, I decided to go to the three-room apartment in Begovaya Street, where he lived with his wife, Fyodor[3], and their daughter Lena. Two of its small rooms were contiguous bedrooms and the third, which was a little larger, served as Grossman's study, as well as the family's dining and living room.

The scene that met me on arrival was Olga Mikhailovna, Zinaida Nikolayevna Pasternak[4], and Bertha Yakovlevna Selvinskaya[5] playing the Chinese game mahjong at a square table in the middle of the room. Grossman and I settled down in the corner while I whispered Nikolai Chukovsky's message. "Repeat," Grossman said. After listening to me for the second

---

1   +Dimunitive of Nikolai.
2   +Lyudmila Skoryno (1908–1999), critic and, in that time, Deputy Chief Editor of *Znamya*.
3   +Olga's son by Boris Guber.
4   +Wife of Boris Pasternak.
5   +Echoing *Life and Fate*.

time, he said, his lips trembling as they always did when he was agitated, "And Lyusya is here playing mahjong." In future years he often recalled that unfortunate game of mahjong, along with Olga's other sins of transgression, both large and small. For example, he believed that his mother, who died in the Berdichev ghetto, would have lived had Olga not been against her joining him in Moscow shortly before the war. But I think Olga was an excellent wife to him. It was just that he stopped loving her in time and fell in love with someone else.

To return to the period after I spoke to Chukovsky about Life and Fate, rumors began to leak from friends who were connected with Znamya. They said that the magazine didn't want to publish the novel. Grossman was finally summoned to an editorial board meeting, which he rightly didn't attend. He received the transcript. Malyuta Skuratovs[1] alternated with Tartuffes at the meeting and unanimously rejected the novel, calling it an anti-Soviet calumny. Nikolai Chukovsky hadn't attended.

Over time, Grossman began to understand that he had made a fatal mistake by entrusting Life and Fate to Kozhevnikov and Krivitsky. He'd tried unsuccessfully to resume relations with Tvardovsky, as appears in the letter he wrote to me in Maleyevka on February 1, 1961, prior to the editorial board's fateful meeting I've just referred to:

Dear Syoma,

I received your letter. O free spirit, poet, and translator! I've been ill again, but this time everything turned out all right, no pneumonia.

Congratulations on your daughter Zoya Semyonovna entering into lawful wedlock. Let the couple know I say, 'God bless them.'

Before I got ill, I had a conversation with

1   +Lukyanovich (a.k.a Malyuta) Skuratov-Beliskiy (d. 1573), one of the most draconian leaders of Ivan the Terrible's Oprichnina (Secret Police).

117

Tvardovsky; we met and talked for a long time. It was a polite conversation, but the outcome weighs heavily. He retreated on all fronts, completely abandoned the manuscript, and distanced himself from all other forms of participation in the literary life of his interlocutor. So that's it.

However, Grossman's relationship with Tvardovsky wasn't wholly fractured. In late Autumn, Grossman went to Koktebel with Olga Mikhailovna and Tvardovsky. Maria Illarionovna[1] was there too. The two men's wives, who'd been neighbors in Chistopol[2], reconciled the husbands after which Tvardovsky said, "Give me the novel to read. Just to read." On his return to Moscow, Grossman took the novel to Tvardovsky along with his secret but unarticulated hopes that *Novy Mir*'s editor would ease its route to publication.

A sober Tvardovsky went to see Grossman as midnight approached on the night the novel was arrested. He said it was brilliant. Then, after having a drink, he cried, "There is no freedom; we cannot tell the truth. What a pity you gave it to the talentless Kozhevnikov. He's good for nothing. I wouldn't have published it, except for some of the battle scenes, perhaps. But I would never have been malicious, you know me."

According to Tvardovsky, Kozhevnikov had passed the manuscript 'to the top.'

Grossman described the evening to me laughing, "As always, there wasn't enough vodka. Tvardovsky was angry, agonized; he said suddenly, 'You intellectuals only think of yourselves – 1937, what Stalin did before that, the collectivization, when he killed millions of peasants, you don't care about that.' Then he started using my own words from *Life and Fate*: 'Sasha, come to your senses …' At first his eyes were confused, then they became vacant, he hung his head, saliva trickled from

---

1   +Wife of Tvardovsky.
2   +During the war.

the side of his mouth."

The arrest took place in February 1961. Grossman called me during the day and said in a strange voice, "Come over now." I realized something terrible had happened, but I had no idea they'd arrested the novel. This had never happened before, as far as I knew. Writers were often arrested, and manuscripts were taken during such arrests but not prior to the arrest of their authors. (I've subsequently learned that in 1926, Bulgakov's manuscript was seized in a similar fashion).

On the morning in question, two plain-clothed men had arrived at Grossman's flat. Olga wasn't at home; she'd gone to the Vagankovsky market. The door had been opened by Natasha, the maid. When the two men entered Grossman's room, Natasha had said to his daughter-in-law Ira, "I think some bad people have come."

The men had handed Grossman a warrant for the seizure of the novel. There was a tall one who had introduced himself as a Colonel. The other, smaller in rank and stature, knocked on Ira's door and said, "Does he have a bad heart? Give him some medicine." Ira had given Grossman some drops and said, "Why have you come?"

"We have to take his novel away. He has written a novel, hasn't he? Now, we'll confiscate it. Don't tell anyone about this. We won't make you sign a written pledge but don't you dare go gossiping."

Then the Colonel's subordinate had gone outside, coming back with what he called two witnesses.[1] Grossman later told me it was apparent they hadn't just been the first available passers-by but were from the same department as his uninvited visitors. A thorough search ensued, with his visitors taking not only the typewritten copy but the original manuscript, the drafts of chapters that hadn't been included in the final manuscript, and all of Grossman's preparatory material, studies, and

---

1   +By Soviet law witnesses were required for searches.

sketches. The men had shown no interest in manuscripts that were unconnected with the novel, such as some stories and the first draft of the novella, *Everything Flows*. They had acted with military precision, performed their mission, and withdrawn only after the novel and all that was associated with it was in their possession. They had only searched the room where Grossman worked. They were polite. The Colonel's subordinate had turned to Grossman and said, "Excuse me for troubling you with a universal need; where's your bathroom?"

The search had lasted over an hour. When it was concluded, the Colonel had asked Grossman if there were other copies elsewhere. To which he'd replied, "At the typist, she kept a copy for herself at home so she could proofread it. There's one at *Novy Mir*. And another at *Znamya*, but you've probably got that one."

They had asked Grossman to promise not to tell anyone about the manuscript's seizure, but he had refused. The Colonel hadn't insisted, and Grossman had been led away. They said to Ira, "Don't worry, he'll be back in an hour and a half; we're accompanying him to the typist."

They not only went to the typist but to Lomonosov Avenue, where Grossman had received temporary lodging through the Writers' Union due to family circumstances. It consisted of a room in a communal apartment. They found nothing there.

When Grossman returned home, he said they had taken the typist's copy. Then it became known that they had gone to *Novy Mir*, ordered that the safe be opened, and taken their copy. I've never seen Grossman as depressed as he was after the arrest of the novel. Boris Yampolsky, whose memoirs I've read in manuscript, accurately describes Grossman's condition when he writes about meeting us both at Alexandrovsky Garden.

I remembered the time in 1953 when *For A Just Cause* was attacked. We had expected Grossman's arrest daily because there was a real danger that he would be linked with the "doctor-murderers" case; he'd suffered less then than he did now. He certainly assumed that after *Life and Fate*, he could be arrested too. But the realization that his most important and most serious work faced a terrible fate tormented him beyond that assumption. "What should I do?" he kept asking, and what could I say to him? I could merely joke bitterly, "Go to the Don and find the white Cossacks," and he had smiled, but the smile had not erased the anguish in his eyes.

Now, as I write this account, I start wondering why it did not occur to Grossman to offer *Life and Fate* to some foreign publisher, say, in a Socialist country, which was more liberal than ours? There was a precedent in the measure of Pasternak's persecution when the Italian Communist publishing house issued the novel *Doctor Zhivago*. Why was Grossman, as he put it, "strangled in the doorway"? Why did the arrest of the novel go unnoticed both in our country and abroad?

These questions are difficult to answer. A possible explanation is that there was limited contact then between Russians and foreign correspondents and editors. In any case, Grossman didn't know any. However, I remember that once, in hospital, a month and a half before his death, Grossman asked me, "Have you read Zhores Medvedev's story of the charlatan Lysenko?"[1] I hadn't. "It's said that Medvedev sent the manuscript abroad, and it came home as a book, and now it's all over Moscow. I was told about this the other day. Do you think I could do that too?"

He didn't wait for my answer but closed his eyes and fell asleep.

As for Grossman's foreign publications, his story 'Life' appeared as a pamphlet in Yugoslavia, something was printed in Poland, and he received a luxury edition of *For A Just Cause* from Czechoslovakia. One of his stories was translated into Chinese, and some work was translated into English, German, and Spanish. All this happened independently of Grossman;

---

1   +The work referred to is by the dissident historian Zhores Medvedev.

he had no contact with the publishers or translators. Even in later years, after *Everything Flows* was published, foreign correspondents never showed any interest in Grossman's fate. They are strange people. We can't understand them, and vice versa.

For all his depression, Grossman did not lose a secret hope that attitudes towards the novel could be changed. He saw both the negative and the positive in Khrushchev and believed his report to the Twentieth Congress of the Party to be remarkable. The Twentieth Congress publications gave Grossman a sketch of optimism. He decided to talk to Dmitry Polikarpov, who'd been the Managing Secretary of the Writers' Union until his career began to wane. Grossman and he spent more and more time in Gagra, where they often met and talked on the beach.

Then Polikarpov's career waxed again, and he became Head of the Central Committee's Cultural Department. I knew him too, he was someone who was only evil when he was ordered to be, but he seemed to forget Gagra's beach, becoming harsh and blunt when he spoke to Grossman. He sighed, "You, a member of the Writers' Union Executive Committee, repeatedly decorated with Soviet orders, look what you wrote!"

He suggested that Grossman write a letter to the Central Committee. If I'm not mistaken, he also advised Grossman to talk to the leaders of the Writers' Union who had read the novel and helped to arrange a meeting when Grossman was able.

Grossman spoke to Markov[1] and Sartakov[2], joint Secretaries of the USSR Writers' Union, and with Shchipachev[3], joint Secretary of the RSFSR Writers' Union and Chairman of the Writers' Union's Moscow branch. According to Grossman, the people he met adopted a harsh tone, but he felt that they disapproved of the arrest of the novel. They acknowledged

---

1   +George Markov (1911-1991), Siberian author, Secretary of the Writers' Union from 1958.

2   +Sergei Sartakov (1908-1993), Siberian author, Secretary of the Writers' Union from 1967.

3   +Stepan Shchipachev (1889-1980), Russian poet.

that it wasn't slanderous and that much of what the author had written was accurate. However, they felt that in the current challenging times, the novel's publication would be bad for our State. They said it might be possible to publish it, but there was no certainty. Schipachev was milder than the others, calling the book "subjective" rather than "harmful."

Grossman wrote a letter to Khrushchev of which I preserved a copy. It was written in the spirit in which, from Pushkin on, all letters to the Emperor had been written. It was full of dignity, fearless faith, bona fides, and belief that the new society was unthinkable 'without the continuous growth of freedom and democracy.' Here's the letter:

> To the First Secretary of the Central Committee of the Communist Party, Nikita Khrushchev.
>
> Dear Nikita Sergeyevich,
>
> In October 1960, I gave the manuscript of my novel *Life and Fate* to the editor of *Znamya*. Around this time, the novel was also read by, Alexander Tvardovsky, the editor of *Novy Mir*. In mid-February 1961, staff members of the Committee for State Security showed me a search warrant and seized from my house all the remaining copies and drafts of the manuscript of *Life and Fate*. The manuscript was also removed from the editorial offices of *Znamya* and *Novy Mir*. In this way, the previous ten-year period, during which I had submitted work to and been repeatedly published by these publications, came to an end.
>
> After the manuscript was removed, I turned to the Central Committee of the CPSU to Comrade Polikarpov. He strongly condemned my oeuvre and advised me to reconsider and acknowledge my book's falsity and harmfulness and write a letter to

the Central Committee admitting I had done so.

A year has passed, and I have thought relentlessly about the disaster that has occurred in my life as a writer and about the tragic fate of my book. I honestly want to share those thoughts with you.

After all this time, I have still not concluded that my book is false. I wrote what I believed and continue to believe is true. I wrote only what I have thought, felt, and suffered through. My book is not political. In it, I wrote, to the best of my limited abilities, about people, their grief, joy, delusions, and deaths. I wrote about love and human compassion. There are bitter, painful pages in it, which address our recent past and the events of the war.

Reading them is probably not easy. But, believe me – writing them was just as hard. However, I could not but write them. I started writing the book before the Twentieth Party Congress during Stalin's time. It seemed then that there was not a shadow of hope I would be able to publish it. But I still wrote it.

Your report to the Twentieth Congress gave me confidence.

I assumed on giving the manuscript to the editor [of *Znamya*] that he would require some pages, maybe even chapters, be edited out.

But when they read the manuscript, the editor, Kozhevnikov, and leaders of the Writer's Union, Markov, Sartakov, and Schipachev, told me that it could not be published, that it was harmful. But even then, they did not accuse the book of being false. One of the comrades said, "All this happened or could have happened. People similar to [the book's] characters existed or could have existed." Another said, "But this book can only be published in 250 years time."

With new clarity, your report to the Twenty-second Congress has highlighted all that was hard and wrong in our country during the time Stalin led us. Your report has further strengthened my conviction that *Life and Fate* does not contradict the truths you have described and that this truth has become a part of today and cannot be postponed for 250 years.

For me, it is especially terrible that my book has been forcibly taken away from me. This book is as dear to me as honest children are dear to their fathers. Taking away my book is the same as taking a child from his father.

My book was confiscated from me a year ago. I have thought incessantly about its tragic fate the whole year and sought to understand what has happened. Is the explanation that my book is subjective?

But then a stamp of the personal, the subjective, is inherent in all works of literature not written by craftsmen. A book by a writer of fiction does not directly illustrate the views of political and revolutionary leaders. It comes into contact with these views, sometimes merges with them, and sometimes contradicts them on certain points. A book, always and necessarily, expresses the inner world of the writer, his feelings, and his intimate images and can not be but subjective. It was always thus. Literature is not an echo. It talks in its own way about life and the drama of life.

Turgenev strongly expressed the Russian people's love for truth, freedom, and goodness, but he was not a proponent of the ideas of the leaders of Russian democracy. His work illustrated life in Russian society in its own way, as did that of Dostoevsky, Tolstoy, and Chekhov. They each expressed good, evil, joy, sorrow, beauty, and the terrible ugliness of Russian life as they saw it. Neither Tolstoy nor Chekhov illustrated the views of those who led the Russian revolutionary democrats, they polished their own mirrors of Russian life, and the mirrors differed from those which created the political leaders of the Russian Revolution. However, neither Herzen, Chernyshevsky, Plekhanov, nor Lenin turned against those Russian writers; they saw in them allies, not enemies.

I know my book is not perfect; it does not compare with the works of the great writers of the past. But the issue is not the weakness of my talent. The issue here is my right to tell the truths I have come to by suffering and maturing through the long years of my life.

I venture to assert that my book may, to some extent, give responses to the internal aspirations of Soviet people; it does not contain lies and slander but does contain truth, pain, and love for people. Why, then, was it banned? Why was it taken from me by forceful administrative methods and hidden from me and from the people – arrested like a criminal murderer?

For the past year, I have been unsure whether my book is still intact, stored, or been destroyed or burned.

If my book is a lie, let this be said to people who want to read it. If my book is a slander, let that be told too. Let the Soviet people, Soviet readers, for whom I have written for 30 years, judge what is true and what is false in my book.

But the reader is unable to judge me and my work at the trial, which is more severe than any other trial, by which I mean the trial which takes place in the heart, the trial of conscience. I wanted and still want this trial.

My book has not only been rejected by the editorial board of *Znamya*, but they even advised me to respond to readers' inquiries by saying I had not finished the manuscript yet, that it would take me a lot longer to do so. In other words, I was asked to lie.

Moreover, when my manuscript was confiscated, I was asked to sign a non-disclosure agreement with criminal penalties was I to breach it.

The methods aimed at keeping secret all that happened to my book were not the methods of dealing with lies and defamation. This is not how lies are combatted. It is how truths are refuted.

What does it mean? How can it be understood in light of the ideas of the Twenty-second Congress of the Party?

Dear Nikita Sergeyevich, it is now often written and said that we are returning to Leninist norms of democracy. At a time of fierce civil war, occupation, economic devastation, and hunger, Lenin created rules of democracy, which during Stalin's era were deemed overly ambitious.

You unreservedly condemned Stalin's bloody lawlessness and violence in your address at the Twenty-second Congress of the Party. The strength and courage with which you did this give me grounds to think that the rules of our democracy will grow, just as the output of steel, coal, and electricity has grown since the collapse that accompanied the Civil War. Indeed, the growth of democracy and freedom, even more than the growth of production and consumption, constitutes the essence of the new society. Without the norms of freedom and democracy continuing to grow, the development of the new society seems unthinkable.

Though full of imperfections, my book was written with the blood of my heart in the name of truth and love for people. How, then, can it be understood that in our time, a writer is searched, his book is taken from him, and he is threatened with jail if he starts talking about his grief?

I am convinced that the most severe and uncompromising prosecutors of my book have, in many ways, changed their points of view. They must recognize as wrong a number of fundamental charges made by them against my manuscripts a year and a half ago, prior to the Twenty-second Congress.

I ask you to give my book its freedom back. I wish my manuscript to be discussed and analyzed by editors, not the people of the Committee of State Security.

There is neither sense nor truth in the present situation or in my physical freedom when the book I gave my life to is in prison. I wrote it, and I did not renounce and do not renounce it. It has been twelve years since I started working on it, and I still consider that I wrote the truth, that I wrote it loving, pitying, and believing in people. I ask for my book's freedom.

With deep respect,
Vasily Grossman.
Moscow, Begovaya street, 1-a, h. 31, apt. 1.
Tel. D-3-00-80. ext: 16.

Grossman hoped that he could convince Khrushchev to return the manuscript even if the book wasn't published. He didn't see "the sense in the current situation." But isn't the power of violence senseless in itself?

There was no immediate answer, but one came relatively soon, after about a month or two, during which Grossman had barely left the house as he was waiting for a phone call. He went out once only to get some air, and that's when they called. Ira picked up the telephone. She was given a phone number and told to ask Grossman to call it as soon as possible. He did so as soon as he got back from his walk. He was invited to attend a meeting with Suslov[1].

They talked for about three hours, and when he got home, Grossman wrote a detailed account of the conversation. He had an excellent memory. The single copy of this account of Grossman's meeting with the 'grey cardinal' was donated on his death, by his widow, to the closed archives of TsGALI.[2] Olga, a simple soul, informed me proudly that General Ilyin, the secretary of the Moscow branch of the Writers' Union, had applauded her action.

Sadly, I can't remember much about this account, which was – as you might imagine – very interesting. Suslov praised Grossman for turning to the First Secretary of the Central Committee and said that the Party and country appreciated parts of his oeuvre, such as *The People Immortal, Stepan Kolchugin*, his war stories, and essays. He went on, "As for *Life and Fate*, I haven't read it, but two of my assistants have. These comrades are well-versed in literature, and I trust them.

"Both, without saying a word to each other, came to the same conclusion, that publication of this work would harm communism, Soviet power, and the Soviet people."

Suslov asked Grossman how he made his living. When he learned that Grossman was going to translate an Armenian

1   +Mikhail Suslov (1902–1982). He was Second Secretary of the Communist Party from 1965. He was the unofficial Chief Party Idealogue, an opponent of reformism.

2   +TsGALI – Central State Archive of Literature and Art, now Russian State Archive of Literature and Art (RGALI). Grossman's archive was released in July 2013 (https://www.rbth.com/literature/2013/08/02/grossmans_life_and_fate_manuscript_has_left_the_secret_archives_28595.htmll)

novel from a version rendered word for word into Russian, he felt sorry for Grossman having to perform this complex two-staged task. He promised to instruct Goslitizdat to publish Grossman's collected works, excluding *Life and Fate* of course. Grossman again raised the issue of releasing his arrested manuscript into his custody. Suslov said, "No, no, that's impossible. We'll issue a collected works, don't even think about this novel. Maybe it'll be published in two or three hundred years."

I don't know if this astronomical time frame traveled up from Suslov's literary functionaries or vice versa. As Suslov spoke, he fingered both of their reviews, looked at their text, and read aloud what he thought were the most objectionable passages of the novel quoted in those reviews. Grossman said the reviews were substantial, estimating that each was about fifteen to twenty pages long.

I recently heard a remarkable detail relevant to this incident from two people who summer in their dachas next door to a former Central Committee Cultural Officer, Igor Chernoustan. Each of his neighbors told me independently that he'd been one of the people who'd reviewed *Life and Fate* and advised it be detained but that Grossman be left untouched.

Suslov's promise wasn't kept, and Grossman's five-volume collected works was never published. Goslitizdat delayed. Grossman complained in a letter to me that its director, Vladykin, "eludes me and avoids replying." In a subsequent letter in late 1961, Grossman wrote to me:

> Today there was a call from *Novy Mir*. Dementyev[1] informed me in an unpleasant manner that they won't be taking the story.[2] Don't congratulate me yet on my collected works; the publishing house's plan hasn't been approved and who's most likely to be cut if there are cuts? I'm on the running board and teetering.

1 *Tvardovsky's deputy at *Novy Mir*.
2 *The story may have been 'Tiergarten' if my memory serves me.

As Grossman predicted, he was cut out of the plan. After his death, as a member of the Writers' Union Commission on Grossman's literary legacy, I discussed his collected works with the new director of the publishing house V A Kosolapov[1] (Grossman had managed to compile and detail the contents of each volume). Kosolapov was receptive to the project and advised me to put forward a proposal to the editorial board's next meeting relating to a five-volume collection of Grossman's work. In the interim, he said I should arrange for prominent writers to send a supporting letter to Goslitizdat, the proposed publisher. The letter was prepared and signed by Ehrenburg, Tvardovsky, and Paustovsky. With Kosolapov's help, Grossman was again included in the editors' preparation plan. Olga Mikhailovna signed a contract for the preparation of the five-volume edition, submitted the first two volumes to the publisher, and even received a small fee, a significant sum to her, but which was, in reality, a small advance. Publication, however, was deferred year after year until the story *Everything Flows* was published abroad, after which, to quote Goslitizdat, the 'publication' was permanently cut out of their plan.

Grossman was aging. His curly hair was becoming increasingly gray, and a bald spot had appeared at the crown. His asthma, from which he'd been reprieved for a while, came back. His gait became a shuffle. His phone was silent, and many of his old friends had gone. He was stung by the behavior of Ruvim Fraerman, the children's writer, who'd been his friend for many years. Grossman wrote to me, "Ruvim called. The conversation lasted a long time, four minutes. Well, at least he called; that's something."

And Grossman needed friends, acquaintances, and people to talk to. What were people afraid of? After all, Stalin was gone. In recent years, I've come to understand Grossman's condition with particular clarity. I experienced something

---

1 +A Kosolapov - editor of *Literaturnaya Gazeta* unil 1962 when he was sacked for publishing 'Babi Yar' by Yevgeneny Yevtushenko.

similar, albeit on a smaller scale, after I left the Writers' Union. Two of my school friends stopped talking to me, I was in my 73rd year, so it's not difficult to estimate how long we'd been friends. I don't even know if they're alive today. It has to be said I've made a number of wonderful new friends. But Grossman didn't have that good fortune. However, in Koktebel, he met Lazar Lazarev, the critic, and Naum Korzhavin[1], the poet, and they were attentive; they understood the significance of his talent. Grossman liked them both but was especially impressed by the poetry of Korzhavin's ideas and the lack of poetry in his demeanor. Grossman was grateful to both for the goodwill they showed him.

Unpublished, excluded from literature, he continued not only to write but also to be keenly interested in everything new that appeared in print. Aksyonov[2] surprised him with his mischievous *Ticket to the Stars*. He enjoyed Voinovich's[3] story 'We Live Here' and Vladimov's[4] *The Great Ore*. He said that those writers had great futures ahead of them. He didn't live to see the famous Chonkin[5], *The Faithful Russian*, *The Burn*, or *The Courtyard in the Middle of the Sky*, but I'm sure Grossman would have appreciated the universality of these great works. He saw the televised evening of poetry at the Luzhniki Stadium and said with great satisfaction that the lively young writers were much more appreciated and by larger audiences than were the official poets dressed in the armor of their rank and position.

Once, he called me and gave me a manuscript with surprising jubilation. It was a story printed, single-spaced, on bible paper. The author wasn't named. The story's title was

---

1 +Naum Korzhavin (1925-2018), a Russian Jewish poet.
2 +Vasily Aksyonov (1932-2009), Russian novelist.
3 +Vladamir Voinovich (1932-2018), Soviet author.
4 +Georgy Vladimov (1931-2003), Ukranian author.
5 +*The Life and Extraordinary Adventures of Private Ivan Chonkin* by Vladamir Voinovich 1969.

a camp prisoner's number. I sat down to read it – and could not break away for a moment from its thin crumpled pages. I read it with joy and pain. Now and then, Grossman came up to me and looked into my eyes, delighted with my enthusiasm. It was *One Day in the Life of Ivan Denisovich*. Grossman said, "You know, all of a sudden, there, in that other world, in penal servitude, a writer is born. And not just a writer, a mature, enormous talent. Who's his equal?"

Grossman learned more about Solzhenitsyn from an employee of *Novy Mir*, Anna Berzer[1]. He wanted to meet Solzhenitsyn and expected that he would call on him. But they were not destined to meet.

Grossman also gave me another manuscript to read that had fallen into his hands, *Within the Whirlwind*. It was written by Evgenia Ginsburg[2]. Grossman praised the writer, who was new to him, said she was very talented and marveled at her powers of recollection.

In his letters to me over the years, Grossman commented on literary works. I think it would be appropriate to quote him.

> I've read Kochetov's novel, *Brothers Yershov*. It's a vile, insignificant product constructed under a plot so primitive it could have been devised in the brain of a rooster, frog, or perch fish. The only consolation is that it's sold 500,000 copies, a mediocre figure. You know, when you're dealing with Hamsun, there's complexity, but here there's none at all; everything's simple and clear. It's like the proverb about bees and their honey.[3]
>
> Have you seen Ehrenburg in January's *Novy Mir*? I read it with interest, a man can wait until he's 70 to

---

1   +Anna Samoilovna Berzer (1900-1996), Literary critic at *Literaturnaya Gazeta* prior to becoming head of fiction at *Novy Mir*.
2   +Evgenia Ginsburg (1904-1977), Russian author who was in a Gulag for 18 years.
3   *Grossman liked this saying: "If the bees are shit, the honey's shit."

be wise, but Ehrenburg is as wise as Mafusail when it comes to what you can write. I've read Lem's book, *Invasion from Aldebaran*. It's rare for a book to give me the anguish this one did. The anguish came, however, not from boredom. The book's interesting, and the author has a spark in his head, but the book makes you feel depressed and disgusted.

I've read Maurois' *The Life of Sir Alexander Fleming*. Read it if you can; it's interesting and, in places, *very* interesting. He's a Scot, and his character is a 'thing in itself', a realistic thing. I read a book by Dutta, *The Philosophy of Mahatma Gandhi*; if you haven't read it, I can lend it to you. I've also read *March* by Yuri Davydov[1]. It's about the Narodnaya Volya[2] people. Read it by all means. It has excellent aspects. He's not a powerful author, but his book has a lot of good in it.

He writes a lot about Plekhanov, and without the qualification, "but." It may be the first time someone's written about Plekhanov without that "but."

At another point he wrote:

I've read a little story by Kazakov[3] in *Ogonyok*[4]. The author's talented; the buzz around him is justified. He's somewhat mannered and strongly influenced by Chekhov, but thank God there is an author still being influenced by Chekhov.

That Elizar Maltsev[5] does not merit that critique.

---

1 +Yuri Davydov (1925-2002), Russian novelist and biographer.
2 +People's Freedom, a late 19th-century revolutionary terrorist organization and successor to the Narodniks.
3 +Yuri Pavlovich Kazakov (1927-1982), Russian Jazz musician turned author.
4 +*Little Flame*, a weekly magazine.
5 +Elizar Maltsev (1917), award-winning Soviet novelist.

I've read a translation of the poem by Tursunzade[1] in *Ogonyok*. The translation was by Semyon Lipkin. Reading it, I remembered the Odesa formula, which I'll paraphrase, 'The form is excellent, but the morality is suspect. How sweetly that cursed Gypsy sings it.'[2]

"I've read Dudintsev[3] in two issues of *Novy Mir*; it's good, brave work, and the business dealings between the characters are realistic. This is important because literature has lost the habit of depicting natural relations between people. He writes of personal relationships, love, and friendship poorly. But I'm grateful, at least for the practical ones; the servants, bureaucrats, and scientists come alive. It is not a matter of talent but about deciding on a type in literature; is it odd or even, black or white, lies or truth.

This work doesn't lie. The fact that Dudinstev is not that talented is a secondary issue only worth discussing when there's a lot more true work being produced. Meanwhile, I'd rather enjoy the images of the prairie and its first creaking wagons as they are conceived, driven by brave pioneers. Good speed, all honor, and the best of luck to them.

I've read a very lovely and light Pasternak poem, 'Being Famous Is Ugly.' If Bor[is] Leon[idovich] thought he wasn't famous for half an hour like another poet we know, he'd 'hang himself on a tree',

---

1 +Mirzo Tursunzode (1911-1977), an important poet and a prominent political figure. Today Tursunzode has been elevated to the level of a national hero of Tajikistan.

2 *Ivan Turgenev's mother's words about Pauline Viardot.

3 +Vladamir Dudinstev (1918-1998), Ukranian author of *Not By Bread Alone* (1956) marking one of the 'Kruschev thaws.'

he wouldn't be able to carry on living.[1] But he came out into the open. His long, arduous path wasn't easy. Good luck to him.

Have you read the Voinovich story in *Novy Mir*? Read it; he has talent, and his talent is truth. Anna Samoilovna spoke about him admiringly.

I'm still reading Yampolsky. A strange thing. Written with style, nice but pointless, like sand.

I recently read Voltaire's 'One must be new without being strange, elevated but always natural.' How well put!

Of course, not all of Grossman's statements about literature were contained in his letters. We met daily unless one of us was away. When we did we talked about literature, people, and many other excellent things, ranging from newly excavated Bactrian Kingdoms to the latest discoveries in physics.

The reader may have been jarred by Grossman's remarks about our great poet Pasternak. I think I'll venture an explanation. Grossman felt and understood the power of poetic expression. In *Life and Fate*, he cites Voloshin's poem, richly saturated with passionate suffering: "My friend, in the death throes ...." He also loved Pushkin, Tyutchev, Lermontov, Nekrasov, and the later poets Bunin and Esenin in their entirety and knew them thoroughly. However, what is now known as 'the magic of language' didn't interest him unless the verse made clear sense, which he felt was essential to people. This explained his attitude toward Pasternak, Mandelstam, and all the poets of the Silver Age, starting from Alexander Blok. He took from them only what his mind and soul needed.

Since I have raised Pasternak, I will recount an episode that relates to him. Somewhere in the mid-fifties, at the Writer's

---

1   *The only poem my youngest son wrote was when he was 12: "If I had seen a tree, I'd have hung myself up on it in no time." These lines made my friends laugh. Akhmatova used to repeat them at difficult times.

House in Dubulti on Riga's coast, we met the writer Davidy Dar[1], a charming man. Dar was Vera Panova's[2] husband. He left Dubulti before us and invited us to Leningrad, promising to book us a room at a hotel. According to him, Panova had long dreamed of meeting Grossman, so we went from Riga to Leningrad, telephoned Dar, and were invited to visit. Panova was highly intelligent and interesting to talk to. Grossman noticed (it was impossible not to) that almost half a wall in her working room was covered with photographs of Pasternak. He was surprised when Panova explained, "Pasternak is my most favorite contemporary Russian poet; he is my idol."

When we took our leave of Panova and Dar's hospitality and walked to the hotel Oktyabrskaya, Grossman said to me with exasperation, "I don't believe her. Who is this 'complex and difficult' Pasternak, this superficial fiction writer to her? She's posing."

A few years later, when Pasternak started being hounded[3] and was going to be excluded from the Writers' Union, Panova came from Leningrad to Moscow to participate, as a Board member, in Pasternak's "procedure of expulsion." "Why?" Grossman raged. "Even Moscow's writers exercised a modicum of decency and stayed at home, explaining that they were sick. While she came from Leningrad to expel her ' favorite poet, her idol.' Remember how Kolya Chukovsky, with his breathy ha ha, ba ba voice recited Pasternak poems to us? Now he takes the floor and adds his voice to his exclusion. Lord, why is your zoo so big?"

Grossman, who was at that time also disenfranchised from Russian culture, wrote to Pasternak. As far as I recall, he didn't touch on Pasternak's tragedy, only wished the poet health and peace with much cordiality.

---

1   +David Jakovlevich Ryvkin (1910-1980), Russian author.
2   +Vera Panova (1905-1973), Russian author.
3   +This refers to the campaign against Pasternak after the publication of *Dr Zhivago* abroad.

I tried to introduce Grossman to Akhmatova for a long time but to no avail. Neither showed any particular desire. I'm not sure that Akhmatova ever read Grossman, though, when he met with one particular misfortune, she asked me about him sympathetically. As for Grossman, I think (although I know this sounds unconvincing) that he became disenchanted with her when he learned from me that she hated Chekhov. Grossman adored Chekhov and knew many pages of his work by heart, including his letters. "How can a Russian writer not love Chekhov?" he said indignantly. Grossman, however, often quoted Akhmatova's lines, such as, "How beautiful you are, the damned one," or "What can the unloved demand anymore?" He understood the charm of her poetry but never discovered its greatness. Akhmatova gave me a copy of the manuscript of her 'Poem Without a Hero.' I called Grossman to my place and read it to him. Then he read it himself, raised his glasses to his forehead, but did not share my enthusiasm.

Grossman, above all contemporary writers, valued Bulgakov, Platonov, Zoshchenko, and Babel. He admired *Sorrow of the Fields* and some stories by Sergeyev-Tsensky[1], especially his 'Bailiff Deryabin.' He appreciated *Ibycus* and *Nikita's Childhood* by Alexei Tolstoy and, as I've mentioned previously, Sholokhov's *Quiet Flows the Don*. He had some surprising passions including a high opinion of Nikandrov's[2] story, 'The First Around the Yard.' He respected Veresayev[3] personally and remembered his novel, *In a Deadlock*. He once asked if I had read Veresayev's translation of *The Iliad*. I said that his version had neither the music nor the power of that made by Gnedich[4]. "You know," Grossman said, "I haven't read *The Iliad*. Have you mastered it?" I replied that as a child, my

---

1   +Sergei Sergeyev-Tsensky (1875-1958), Russian author.
2   +Nikolai Nikandrov (Shevtsov) (1878-1964).
3   +Vikenty Veresayev (1867-1945), Russian author and doctor.
4   +Nikolay Gneditch (1784-1833), Ukrainian poet known for translating *The Iliad*.

favorite books after the Bible were *The Iliad* and *The Odyssey* and that Tolstoy had studied ancient Greek to be able to read it in the original. Some time later, he shared with me his own impressions of reading *The Iliad*. It fascinated him. "We rush to read contemporaries; will any of them endure? *The Iliad*'s alive; it surrounds us."

Grossman liked *Russia Washed in Blood* by Artyom Vesely[1] and *The Embezzlers* by Kataev[2]. He believed that the brilliant Kataev missed his true vocation for the sake of commercial gain.

Stern, direct, uncompromising, demanding, ascetic, like a literary Franciscan, Grossman watched with sadness and anger as significant talents such as Alexei Tolstoy gradually compromised themselves. Those he felt weren't divinely gifted but merely literarily skilled, he spoke of with neither bitterness nor contempt.

He'd listen with curiosity and focus to my stories about the writers I'd known who'd died in Stalin's time, Mandelstam, Babel, Bulgakov. I knew Marina Tsvetaeva, although much less well than the others, and I told him I first met her in the early years at her friend, the poetess Vera Zvyagintseva's house. Marina wanted to see me because she was editing the French translation of a chapter from the Kalmyk epic, Jangar, which I had translated into Russian.

Then in late November or early December 1940, I spent a memorable day with her from nine in the morning until late at night. After that, I didn't see her again; we just talked on the phone a few times.

Interestingly, Grossman found Tsvetaeva (who was even more hermetic than Pasternak) closer to his soul than the transparent Akhmatova. Grossman, who stubbornly followed Voltaire's maxim, "One must be new without being strange,"

---

1   +Artyom Vesely (1900-1938), Russian author who was shot for leading anti-Soviet terrorist groups.
2   +Valentin Kataev (1897-1986), Russian author.

would say of Tsvetaeva, "It's simple, [she] just asks, 'My dear, what have I done to you?' Simply, powerfully." It's possible that he admired how open Tsvetaeva was, her offensive fury, the violence with which she tore away syntactic veils.

It's hard not to tell some of my stories here, if only because I remember Grossman's reactions to them so vividly. An example is a story I told him about a time when I was out with Tsvetaeva, walking for hours in Zamoskvorechye. I mentioned how her raincoat had seemed too thin for the time of year and that, while eating at a basic workers' café close to the museum on Gritsevets Street, she'd shown me a review by Zelinsky of her collection for *The Soviet Writer*. It had been so vile in its entirety that the publisher had decided only to show Marina Ivanovna a part of it.[1]

When I eventually told Grossman all this, his eyes shone under his horn-rimmed spectacles, and he said, "Terrible, that son-of-a-bitch Zelinsky didn't act alone in this. You know what little things portend, something monstrous, a raincoat in winter, sauerkraut soup. Tsvetaeva, a delicate, refined poet, and the Metrostroy canteen.

"I think the fates of Tsvetaeva and Akhmatova were much harder than that of Princess Volkonskaya.

"They and those like them are people about whom a new 'Russian Women'[2] should be written. Would you try it?"

Another story I told Grossman was about when I was eighteen years old and recently settled in Kuntsevo near Bagritsky, who had found me a den. I usually spent my evenings at his place. One day in April 1930, Babel arrived at Bagritsky's. It was the first time that I'd seen him. He was a short, thickset man with wise rabbinic eyes. From what he said, I realized he'd been out of Moscow a long time, in a distant

---

1   This story appears in its entirety from page 35
2   *N A Nekrassov (1821–1877) wrote a cycle of poems called 'Russian Women.' It was dedicated to the 'Decembrists' including Princess Volkonskaya who followed their husbands to Siberia.

village. I heard him say something I will remember forever: "Believe me, Edward Georgiyevich, I've learned to watch calmly when people are shot."

Grossman felt sorry for Babel, not only because he died so young and was killed by them but also because this clever, gifted, high soul had uttered those insane words. He asked me what had happened to Babel's soul? Was it true he had celebrated New Year with the Yezhov[1] family? Why? Why was it that extraordinary people like him, Mayakovsky, and my Bagritsky, were so attracted to the GPU?

Were they fascinated by strength and power? Why had Babel associated with shady characters at the racetrack, under Kozhevnikov's surveillance? Grossman felt this grave, terrible phenomenon was something we should think about.

Another story I told Grossman took place during the 'Great Break' when the almanac *The Depth* was published in Moscow. It was strange, full of 'Smiths'[2], strictly proletariat, worker-authors like Gladkov, Novikov-Priboy, Lyashko, Bakhmetyev, Veresayev, Zamyatin, Bulgakov and the tall mustachioed Nikiforov, known by everyone as 'Zhora' (who looked like an actor playing a worker in a B-movie and still ended up getting arrested). On the recommendation of its poetry editor, Sergey Obradovic[3], the periodical agreed to print a weak, pretty early poem of mine about the death of a rural newspaper correspondent in Odesa who was murdered by his jealous brother.[4] The press suggested the murder depicted was ideological, that its motive was class hatred. When I arrived at the editorial office (which was in a dilapidated old house in Varvarka

---

1   +N Y Yezhov (1895-1940), Chief of the GPU (State Political Directorate) arrested and executed in 1940. The 'Great Terror' of 1937-1938 has been called the 'Yezhovschina' in recognition of the leading role he played in it.
2   +This group of proletarian writers referred to themselves as 'The Smiths.' They were active from 1920-1931.
3   +Sergey Obradovic (1892-1956), Russian Soviet poet.
4   +Lipkin was studying engineering at this time.

Street), its secretary, the 'blacksmith' Dmitriev, said it hadn't been approved by the censor and asked if I'd like the proof as a souvenir. That was how I was first exposed to censorship at age nineteen. I was confused and didn't know what to do. Should I leave or stay?

At the back of the room sat a man whose face seemed beautiful, significant, unusual, and un-Soviet; it had something of the old life. He looked at me, jerked his head to the side which made me feel he was somehow unhappy with me. Could it be because of the censor forbidding my poem? I found out later he had a nervous tic. He wore an old crumpled jacket, which was both tight and short on him, a frayed, 'ancien regime' snow-white shirt with a starched front, its cuffs protruding from his jacket sleeves, and a bow tie. "Chin up, my young poet," he said. "You start your career in the best Russian tradition, with the censor against you." This was the gracious Mikhael Afanasyevich Bulgakov, who invited me to dine with him at the Actors' House at Strastnaya. As we headed to Nogin Square to take the number fifteen tram, I said, with subtlety, of the big black crowd in the square, "It looks as though there hasn't been a tram for a long time." He answered me with, "I'm unsurprised when trams don't run on time; the surprise is when they do."

He often reminded me of this joke. Neither of us knew his novel *The Master and Margarita*, but Grossman always saw Bulgakov as a miracle of Russian literature. He'd say, "Think about it, Gabrilovich was his neighbor in Nashchokinskoye, they shared a balcony, separated by a partition, but he never tried to talk to Bulgakov. It seems he had more interesting things to do, superficial things."

When something obscure happened, Grossman would always say, "I'm unsurprised when trams don't run on time, the surprise is when they do."

Despite the novel's arrest, sad circumstances in his personal life, financial difficulties, and declining health, Grossman continued to work every day. "Graphomaniacs are obstinate," he would say. He wrote several excellent stories, only some of which have been published. He rewrote the novella *Everything Flows*, almost doubling its length.

A tape recording of Grossman reading one of his stories has been preserved. And we, his close friends, play it on his birthday, December 12, so we can hear his voice. The story is called 'In the Big Ring.' The story turns on Grossman's impressions of a girl based on the daughter of his university friend, Vyacheslav Loboda[1]. It is set in a dacha outside Moscow. The protagonist is the daughter of highly intelligent parents. She is brought up hearing talk of 'Dmitri' (Shostakovich) and 'Lev Davidovich' (Landau). She clearly loves her father, a seemingly clever, ironic, renowned art expert. When she has a sudden attack of appendicitis and is taken to the nearby country hospital, she sees a very different side of life. To one side of her, the old woman in the bed is old, foul-mouthed, angry, but also very kind – a bit like Grossman. On the other side, the protagonist is flanked by a young, single, pregnant woman who works at a construction site and doesn't exactly know who her baby's father is. This protagonist, who hails from deep in the Soviet establishment, hears plenty of things that teach her how life's truth is rough, poor, and unfair. That reality isn't what she finds at home but is there in that rural hospital. She hears, among other things, the following story about two pregnant women in a hospital who give birth on the same day, one the wife of a lieutenant from a nearby military base and the other a simple girl whose baby's father won't marry her. The lieutenant's wife doesn't want to feed her baby because she wants her breasts to stay beautiful, so both babies are suckled by the simple girl. The lieutenant finds out, and when the mothers are due to be discharged, he takes the simple girl and both babies home rather than his wife. After hearing this story and seeing life in the hospital, the daughter in 'In the Big Ring' herself

---

1   +To whom Grossman entrusted a copy of his manuscript *Life and Fate* (1961) which only came to light after its publication in the West.

goes home, her perspective changed. She now sees her art-expert father and the people she knows as shallow, callous, and mendacious. It's a poignant story, which should be published, and appreciated firsthand rather than through my attempts at a sketch.

I can see Grossman walking Puma, his poodle, in the evenings. Sometimes the dog breaks away from him as he stands in one place for a long time, looking into other people's ground-floor windows. His literary curiosity wasn't bound by convention. When we went to a party, he loved to go into the communal kitchen. He wanted to know what was happening in the bowels of the apartment, at its rear, concealed from guests. Similarly, when he went to Armenia, his book *Dobro Vam* described its courtyards because he said they exposed "human life, the heart's tenderness, rage, and blood ties."

One day, a dark, dumpy Armenian woman called Hasmik (I've forgotten her surname) told me that she had translated a remarkable Armenian war novel by Hrachya Kochar. But Kochar considered it literal rather than literary (rightly, as it turned out). Hasmik said it needed editing by a war veteran if possible. She asked if I could recommend somebody and said there'd be an invitation to Armenia for them. The Republic would cover travel expenses, and a local publisher would sign the contract. I thought it would be nice for Grossman to go to Armenia, and he would welcome the fee[1]; he needed money desperately at that time. So I suggested Grossman to Hasmik. Later, in *Dobro Vam*, Grossman portrayed Hasmik as Hortense (which means 'jasmine' in Armenian).

I wasn't sure how Grossman would take the suggestion; even when he needed money, Grossman didn't like commissions. Long ago, when he was surprised by the attack on his play, *According to the Pythagoreans*, he said to his wife, "What should I do now?" Olga said, "Write scripts." He never forgave

---

1   +Robert Chandler's comment from *An Armenian Sketchbook* (MacLehose Press, 2013).

her. To my recollection, he only accepted a commission once when the Vakhtangov Theater asked him to write a play. He dramatized one of his war stories. The central character was an old school teacher, Rosenthal, who believed exterminating Jews had been a product of "the arithmetic of atrocity rather than of spontaneous hate ... and that the accountants had been wrong." I thought the play was clever and sad and had been well adapted for the stage, but the theatre rejected it. By 1947 writing on Jewish themes was already taboo. Grossman gave the play, which he'd called *The Teacher*, to Solomon Mikhoels, who loved it, and it was translated into Yiddish.

I knew Mikhoels well (I'd been introduced to him before the war by Samuel Galkin, in whose poetic translation the Mikhoels' Yiddish theatre had staged *King Lear*). Grossman and I visited Mikhoels several times in his apartment near the old TASS building[1]. The ideas Mikhoels conceived for Grossman's play exposed a brilliant mind and a subtle natural sense of theatre. We drank cherry brandy, which Mikhoels' wife had made herself. As far as I know, she was the only representative of the Polish aristocracy in Russia.

We went with Mikhoels on his penultimate journey (he was going to Minsk on a minor matter to see a play nominated for the Stalin Prize). I remember being on that Belarussian station platform. I remember Mikhoels' big ugly face, his eyes, like a Kabbalist's, like a sorcerer's, his lower lip, which protruded sardonically, the magnificence of his Russian, the theatricality of his slow diction, as he said, "I'm sure that I'll play *The Teacher*. It will be my last role." Veniamin Zuskin[2], another great actor, was there, and he, Grossman, and I waved goodbye to Mikhoels.

He didn't play the last role as he expected to – on stage. Instead, like the hero in Grossman's play, he was murdered.

---

1 +The Telegraphic Agency for the Soviet Union which collected and distributed all news for Soviet media.

2 +Veniamin Zuskin (1899–1952), the people's artist of the RSFSR in 1939.

In that dark Minsk night, Mikhoels was hit by a truck, killed by the same force which killed Rosenthal, the teacher in Grossman's play.

We had seen Mikhoels off on his last earthly journey. Now we moved with the large crowd amassed on Tversky Street and the side streets which led to the VTO building where Mikhoels lay in his coffin, to Malaya Bronnaya, which housed GOSET, the Jewish State Theater. The State buried Mikhoels very differently from the way it buried the poets, writers, and actors who were his friends.[1]

Mikhoels' real name was Vovsi. He was a cousin of the famous doctor Vovsi, a professor who was one of the main accused among the "doctor-murderers." Professor Doctor Vovsi was released after Stalin died. He survived his ordeal.

I hope it's not unacceptable to have digressed from the Armenian to the Jewish question and back again. Grossman was interested when I suggested he travel to Armenia, and he said, "If the novel isn't mean, I'll translate it. Well paid, you say? That's good. I need the money, and my spirits are low, maybe this piece work will be good for me."[2]

Hasmik brought Grossman the large manuscript containing her word-for-word translation of the novel. Grossman was satisfied as to its caliber, only asking, "Are literals always this illiterate?" He took the train to Armenia in November and often wrote to me from there. I want to acquaint the reader with some of those letters. It is interesting to compare Grossman's last book *Dobro Vam* with his impressions of Armenia before they made it into his fiction. What life force is

1   +Refers to the victims of the anti-cosmopolitism campaign.
2   +Yury Bit-Yunan has questioned the reliability of this recollection of Lipkin's, given his projections as to Grossman's earnings during those years. He also puts forward the account of Mary Kochar, Hrachya Kochar's daughter, which implies that it was The Vardes Tevekelyan as opposed to Lipkin, who made the introduction between Grossman and Kochar. Yury Bit Yunan, 'Vasily Grossman and Hrachya Kochar' in Vasily Grossman, *An Armenian Sketchbook*, pp. 197–207.

contained in the letters of the writer who'd been "strangled in a doorway." I quote these letters in full, save for when they relate to purely personal matters.

4th November 1961

Dear Syoma,

I've come to Armenia. I think you, above all, would feel with particular force what constitutes this amazing country's soul, its compound of incredible rigors, its rocky land, blue basalt, millennial churches, and its coterminous of ancient and modern life. I think you'd sense the surprising depth, the wholly biblical past and landscape mixed with contemporaneity, its southern, dark, hard, and noisy life, its incredible labor of peasants cutting bread out of basalt, and its powerful Yerevan hardheads, which chime with initiative. God, if you only knew how many Armenians there are in Yerevan!

Kochar was supposed to have met me at the station, but I got the train's arrival time wrong and found myself alone. I remembered the description you gave as you built up our arrival in Tbilisi: "There'll be speeches, children with bouquets, a band; Grossman will like that. Grossman doesn't like it quiet ....."[1]

So I stood on the empty platform feeling somewhat better, handed my goods and chattels to the left luggage, and got on a bus to look for Kochar. What can I say here except that I like it?

---

1 *In 1956 Grossman and I toured from Moscow, Nalchik, Makhachkala, Baku, Tbilisi to Sukhumi. We were well met everywhere but Baku, where I didn't have connections. We couldn't get an hotel, and so went straight on to Tbilisi. Grossman was upset, and so on the train I devised and played out this anticipatory scene of the grand welcome he'd get in Tbilisi.

Georgia was warm and green; we drove through Gori, where there was a huge portrait of Stalin in his marshal's uniform flanked by modest portraits of Lenin and Khrushchev. Tbilisi's station was cheerful and lively. The windows weren't glazed. Yerevan is nice too, the beautiful pink rendered houses, the grand square. But it doesn't have Tbilisi's charm.

Stalin's statue, military-coated, stands on a hill and looms over the city. The monument's dimensions and prominence give it some mystical, superhuman power. Kochar took me to Lake Sevan today. But you know, the Issyk-Kul remains more magnificent; the mountains around it are whiter.[1] But then, at the Issyk-Kul, there is no restaurant like Minute, where you're served freshly caught pink trout. Tomorrow, as I promised you, I'll go to Etchmiadzin, the residence of Armenia's Catholics. I will write to you about it. I'm living in a small first-floor room with a bathroom, and, forgive me, my own WC.[2] I'll probably go to work in someone's holiday place near Yerevan on the 10–12th.

9th November 1961

... I'm living in Yerevan, a city I love. The weather's good, it's warm and sunny in the afternoons, and it rains at night. The rain was so heavy that first day that I thought how good it was that Mount Ararat was so near. I see it in front of my window. It's pink in the morning, shines white in the afternoons, and is

---

1   *In 1948, we traveled to Kyrgyzstan and visited the mountain lake Issyk-Kul. Grossman wrote about this trip in an essay.

2   *Sholokhov in his speech at a party convention called for writers to elevate the creative spirit by leaving the capital with its sanitary facilities and going to live in rural areas.

pink again in the evenings. Sometimes it disappears in the smoke clouds of Yerevan's factories. I went to Etchmiadzin, where the churches of deep antiquity have survived till today. Of course, they've been restored. Their architecture is amazingly simple. Under the main cathedral, which still operates, hidden in the ground, there's a pagan first-century church, and directly under its altar, there's a scary, dark copper pagan altar. And while I was in the church, a young Armenian priest baptized a girl.

I was received by the Catholicos, Vasgen the First, in his Patriarchal chambers. He's about fifty, worldly, in his black silk robe, with kind, beautiful eyes and lips like Gabrielle de Coignard's, which like to 'praise the Lord in his creations.' The Catholicos drank a glass of brandy to my health. We talked about literature and had black coffee. We were served by a monk, an incredibly handsome young man. Vasgen the First's favorite author is Tolstoy, who the Church anathematized. Vasgen has written a work on Dostoevsky; he told me that man couldn't be understood without Dostoevsky. It went well and was interesting, but I did not see God in Etchmiadzin.

Meals are served with lots of spicy condiments. Everybody drinks three-star cognac. Market prices are as high as Moscow's, and fruit is expensive. But the stores are full of food.

I saw a fight; a young Armenian wanted to hack a fat lady to death, as well as a woman who was obviously his wife. He was surrounded by old women, but he still raised his axe to them. It all ended without bloodshed, but there was lots of shouting. And it happened against the backdrop of Mount Ararat. You can imagine the uniqueness of the experience, the snowy holy mountain, and an impassioned axe-wielding man with a black hat.

I'm working. I can't follow your advice in this respect; I'm very tense; I rush and rush at it without rest. And I have very sad moments, a lot of memories ...

I'll interrupt my Grossman quote to say a few words about Vazgen (who Grossman refers to as Vosgen). I later had the honor of being introduced to the Catholicos of all the Armenians when I went to Etchmiadzin in the Spring of 1972, together with Inna Lisnyanskaya[1]. One day he received Lolita Torres, a famous actress from Latin America, at the same time as us. The Catholicos spoke Spanish with her and German with me. He said that we'd done the right thing in coming to Armenia on the sad anniversary of the 1915 genocide. He fascinated us with his affability, intelligence, and the kindness with which his beautiful eyes shone. Unlike Grossman, I saw in him a man of deep and simple faith. True religious feeling is always discernable in any such encounter.

He told us exactly when he was to proceed to the church and invited us to follow him, enabling us to break through the crowd. And so the Catholicos, accompanied by the Armenian Church's hierarch, all in purple robes, walked down the long corridor, and we, his unknown guests, followed behind.

The prayer commemorating the dead began. During worship, the Catholicos was silent, and the sermon was delivered by an extraordinary priest of noble beauty. I'll never forget the harmonious polyphonic singing of the choir. I felt a sense of connection to eternal truth, the triumph of victims' survival over that of executioners. Inna Lisiyanskaya, Armenian on her mother's side, cried and crossed herself. No one else in the church wept.

When the service was over, a small, thin Armenian woman who had come from the U S threw herself at the feet of the

---

1   +The author's wife, a baptized Christian.

Catholicos. He blessed her. Everyone went out of the church happy and enlightened. There was no despondency but rather a joy of human communality, a kind of children's joy. The crowd in the square parted before the Catholicos, mothers reached out to him with their children, and he blessed them. It was one of the most glorious moments in my life. I wrote a poem, 'The Anniversary of the Armenian Grief', in which I spoke of humanity's universal church.

Returning to Grossman's letters:

15th November 1961

This afternoon and evening, after sunset, no one's wearing a coat, the weather's mild, clear, wonderful. The sycamores are gold ... I'm working hard – the driver drives the horses! I'm still living in Yerevan, but I'll move to the writer Kochar's house near Yerevan in a few days. I don't know how that'll feel; it's pretty high up. We'll start typing the first volume there.

I don't feel entirely well, but I may be improving. I went on two wonderful trips, to the ruins of the pagan church of Garni (which is 2000 years old) and to the rock cave church of Gegard. These rock churches are impressive. Imagine tunnels pierced into solid rock, and from the tunnel inside the rock, they built a church. It has an altar, columns, and a dome; everything's perfect, and everything's made in stone. Only faith could have created this masterful vision inside a stone mountain. Even 'Remember the master' is carved in stone in ancient Armenian letters. And standing near the entrance, an old priest in a black cassock sells postcards, one of which I'm sending to you.

The priest comes from Palestine, has served at the Armenian Church in Jerusalem. There he is among the basalt stones smiling with kind brown eyes. The entrance to the church is splattered with fresh blood: the believers make sacrifices there, slaughtering lambs and chickens.

I visited the library of old manuscripts, and they showed me such wonders; a thousand-year life of thought, word, and paint. There are also ancient Jewish manuscripts and works of the Armenian David the Invincible, so named because he won the debate with the Greeks. Six hundred calves were killed to make one particularly enormous book.

Today Yerevan's alive and noisy. In the morning, I eat breakfast in the hotel café, usually at 8AM, a curd pancake, while my swarthy cousins eat an early barbecue, and instead of tea, defy decorum and start the day with a little bottle of cognac. The city is European in many ways, the main streets are bright, but sheep are driven to slaughter through the cars, past the luxury Intourist hotel and the Council of Ministers building. They go willingly; their hooves clatter while women's heels clatter next to them, and local boys stroll. And near the prosecutor's office, next to the hotel, stand sad fat old men and women with grief in their eyes, the relatives of outlaws.

As for the experience of Zvyagintseva and Petrovykh[1], I concur [on their work's value] with my limited knowledge of them, Comrade Technical Quartermaster![2] I think one must be able to ask, can Armenia contain all its Alikhanyans and

---

1   *Vera Zvyagintseva and Maria Petrovykh are Russian poets who translated from Armenian.

2   *Grossman often called me this after I'd read him my poem, 'The Technical Lieutenant-Quartermaster' (which he also provided the title for). [See *A Close Reading of 53 Poems by Semyon Izrailevich Lipkin* translated by Yvonne Green and Sergei Makarov (Hendon Press, 2023)].

Hambartsumyans?[1]

My Jewish heart is delighted by the bazaars, especially their mountains of fruit and vegetables – Ararats of eggplants, quince, peppers, apples, and pomegranates. The sickly-sweet grapes are amber-colored. Radish prevails; there are mounds of them; some weigh 40 pounds and are 30 inches long. They are strong, red, and thick, these quaintly phallic products of horticultural commerce.

In the evening, I turn on Armenian radio. Not the voiced-over Moscow commentary's indistinct accent but music. In the early morning, I come up to the window to look for Mount Ararat. It's dark, the sparrows shout very loudly. Armenian sparrows are the noisiest I've ever heard. A narrow Turkish moon shines in the sky.

From Kozma Prutkov's[2] observations, I can share the following: many residents, even the most well-dressed, scratch their backsides in the street, maybe because they're hirsute.

Well, now, my dear, I've done as you asked and written more about my Yerevan life, and even if I digressed, I've jabbered with you all night, almost like we do in Moscow … I'm sorry that Akhmatova is so ill …

22nd November 1961

I've been living for four days in a wood cutter's lodge up in the mountain village of Tsakhkadzor, about

---

1   *Hambartsumyan - One of the founders of theoretical astrophysics who's further translated *The Illiad* into Armenian.

2   *Kozma Prutkov was a 19th century humorous Russian conceit, produced by a group of authors. He was a stupid, vain official, sure of his genius. The group's principal author was a brilliant poet Alexei Konstantinovich Tolstoy, (1817-1875).

an hour's drive from Yerevan. It's a beautiful village, the houses, courtyards, everything clings to the mountainside. But the weather is terrible; it's pouring day and night, cold rain mixed with grainy snow. The clouds are on the mountains; they close them in. They say it can rain like this for a month. There's almost no rain in Yerevan, and it's much warmer. I work hard from morning until late at night. I'm exhausted. In the evening, not a single thought remains, only fatigue.

Kochar and his wife are also staying here. They go to Yerevan almost every day to celebrate weddings; there are so many of them. Then the fat Hasmik arrives. She's put on 100 pounds while Grossman, the translator, has put on 16; he now weighs 210 pounds. What does he eat, you ask? Barbecued trout, which comes from Sevan in a bucket, sweet-scented herbs, string cheese, yogurt, radishes, yogurt soup, lavash[1], and sour cream. My diet's good and generally as varied as that of one of Moscow Zoo's orangutans. But I'm not gaining weight; my temperament's obviously to blame. Stupidly I didn't bring a black suit, although I was advised to. And it turns out that in Yerevan, black is the favorite color; everyone respectable goes out in a black suit.

The first two days, the weather in Tsakhkadzor was good, and I took long walks; I liked it very much here. The town's built of stone, and there's a deserted Thirteenth Century church that is amazingly light and simple. There are blood and chicken feathers on the rocks; believers sacrifice cows, calves, sheep, and donkeys on the pavement there. You don't see many people, but old and young greet you and smile; children are sweet, lively, and winsome. Clothes are

---

1   +A flatbread.

dried on lines across courtyards at night. They say there are no thieves. In the yards, bearded Molokans[1] live alongside Armenians. Each has a copper samovar; generally, people drink 25–40 glasses of tea a day. Molokans set up their samovars at weddings. Tsakhkadzor's Molokans aren't from the jumper set who live mainly in Yerevan.

For the last two days, it's poured constantly. The Kochars have gone to another wedding, and fat Hasmik has gone with them, so I'm alone in a large two-story house on a hill. Somewhere below is old Hovhannes, the night watchman. His son's been convicted of murder; he killed a man in a fight.

Hovhannes is big-nosed, unshaven, and doesn't know Russian, but when I pass by, he lifts a finger and laughs, 'They left you alone, didn't take you to the wedding.' Among Armenians, one often meets people with gray eyes or blue eyes. All Russians speak excellent Armenian, but many Armenians don't speak Russian, and if they do, for the most part, it's broken.

As I write to you, the rain's buzzing, and an hour ago, there was thunder.

Thank you for writing out that long passage from *Inostrannaya Literatura* [*Foreign Literature*]. It was a surprise, vivifying. After all these weeks here, I'd forgotten my former occupation. Perhaps that's why I'm working from morning till night and getting so tired, harassing myself with craft. But then they feed me with trout …

26th November 1961

Today I went to Yerevan and collected some mail.

---

1   +A religious sect.

It was warm there though people wore jackets, and the plane trees were still golden. In Tsakhkadzor, the snow creaks under my feet, and children sled and ski.

Semushka, dear, how beautiful all this is; countless sheep wandering in white snow, a milky haze in the blue sky, sugar mountains, and Mount Ararat soaring above the clouds, its white head shining.

I'm glad they're making a TV program about your book of translations, write to me about how it goes, don't forget.

Are you really going to Kazan before the 18th of December? You know, I can't stand it when you are away, although I'm away in Yerevan myself now. But it seems you'll only be gone for 2–3 days, which is tolerable.

I received a letter from my Moscow editor Ivanova saying my book[1] will go through without delay. It is a sweet letter, but she wants to remove the same four stories Fyodor Levin[2] and Vera Panova had a bash at in their reviews. What's left to report? Like a peasant from *Who's Happy in Russia*, I can say, "... Yes, we were beaten by Kalashnikov."[3] I'm no longer varying my routine and having new experiences. I've stopped going away. I sit from morning to night at my table, don't go out to dine, and I get tired.

And at the same time, I'm experiencing very different impressions (or rather thoughts) about the nature of things and people – you know, like

---

1   *A small collection of short stories *The Old School Teacher* was with difficulty published by Sovetsky Pisatel' (Soviet Writer) in 1962.

2   +Fyodor Levin (1901-1972), Jewish literary critic, expelled from the Party for 'cosmopolitanism.'

3   *N A Nekrasov (1821-1877). Grossman is paraphrasing Nekrasov's poem 'Who Can Be Happy in Russia' in which Savely actually says, "... we were flogged by Shalashnikov."

Chekhov wrote in his notebook, in the article enti-
tled 'Turgenev and the Tigers' ....

11th December 1961

... You ask about my affairs. My work has moved
forward considerably, and I think I'll complete it by
the end of December, though meeting deadlines is not
just up to me but also the typists. I've finished dealing
with the horribly illiterate word-by-word translation
and reached the last of its 1420 pages.[1] I'll read and
edit the manuscript once it's typed.

Despite the literal's shortcomings, I've already
had the first 100 pages.

The manuscript's as close to the original as
Gorokov's *Market* after Krasnoarmeyets edited it
for the Red Army in October 1942. My soul is liter-
ally resting. I've just understood the wisdom of the
story advising you to take a goat into your house if
you've got problems.[2] It is bliss once you can put the
goat out again, but it's still on my porch. What will
happen when it's out of the house, and I go to the
seaside for 2 or 3 weeks? Maybe I'll say I'm bored
inside without the goat. No, no, that won't happen.
It's clear to me that I want to go back to my own
broken trough.[3]

I'm almost used to the author's sleepy and indif-
ferent attitude to the fact that an elderly man is
working on this book with such zeal that in the

1   +Arus Tadeosyna's literal translation of *The Children of the Large House*
(Sovetsky Pisatel', 1955), published in 1956 (Voenizdat).
2   +Refers to Jewish Folklore.
3   +The image from Alexander Pushkin's *Tale of The Fisherman and The Fish*
(Biblioteka dlya chteniya, 1835) means: to be left with nothing; to be back
where one started; but also, in Grossman's case, to return to his ruined literary
fate.

evening, his face and forehead are covered with purple spots. A fortnight ago I was shocked by this, but now I'd be shocked if I ever heard a word of thanks.

However, speaking practically, the food's good, the lodgings clean and warm, payments regular, and the bed linen's changed every seven days. I mustn't grumble. I'm not grumbling ...

I've become an old-timer here. I say hello to about a dozen people. Breathing's easy; this is a perfect place for a walk in the morning. The sky's blue, and you go along a mountain road and see sheep, forests, monasteries, and chapels on the mountainsides. You meet an old man, smile, and say, "Barev dzez (good to you)." You know, Armenians have been Christian since the fourteenth century, but it seems to me that they are really pagans, good, hard-working, hot-tempered pagans. I don't feel anything Christian ...

12th December 1961

... The other day we went to Dilijan. After a person turns 55, he should live in Dilijan, though it's a good place once you're 50, too, just right. Lord, what beauty! Away from the railroad, in a mountain hollow, amid pines, there are huts surrounded by open-air terraces which cling to the mountain's slope. What a world, what silence. They say air heals cardiac patients and asthmatics. The route to Dilijan goes past Lake Sevan, via mountains, and through the Semenov Pass. En route, there are snowy peaks, pines, Armenians, Molokans, sheep, donkeys, and mountain streams.

It was only a short rest. I continue to work very

hard so EBZ[1], I'll finish the job in December. I've started receiving the copy from the typists; my client read it with a sour face, but I think it's all right. A big job's been done in good faith. I'm annoyed and upset by my client's restraint; the least he could do is thank the worker. But after all, this is just an episode in my life, a spent life. Like I told you, "I was beaten by Kalashnikov." What thanks can I expect?

I am glad I can relax now. I'm fatigued from so much sitting at the table. It's not just my mind that's tired; my face has spots on it, and my back and shoulders ache. I'm hoping I'll have a good rest after this hard labor, but after reading the article that Zhorzhik Munblit[2] wrote about me, I feel like I've been eaten by a cockroach. Is there a Jewish word that means cockroach? From that cockroach Ruvim, there's no news. Did he call you, or is he still keeping his distance? He makes me feel like eating a cockroach. Fraerman-Cockroach and I were friends for a quarter of a century. Never mind, "I was beaten by Kalashnikov."

25th December 1961

I'm back in a hotel in Yerevan, having said farewell to the beautiful Tsakhkadzor (which means 'Valley of Flowers'). It turns out it's impossible for me to stay in the mountains during the last stage of this work because I have to deal with the publisher and the editor.

I hope by the end of the month I'll be finished

---

1   *EBZ, in Russian, is short for "Esli Budu Zhiv" ["If I'm still alive"] and was a favourite saying of Leo Tolstoy.

2   *Refers to Georgy Munblit's article about Grossman in *The Literary Encyclopedia*.

with everything, although I fear I'll be held back by delays in payment, without which, as you can easily understand, I can't get to Sukhumi ... I hope if there is any delay, it's brief, no more than a couple of days.

In the evening, before leaving Tsakhkadzor, I had another great experience. I visited the Molokan village community elder. He is an old bearded man, and his face emanates a bright, clear feeling. Vasgen the First, educated, enlightened, brilliant Catholicos of all the Armenians, is nothing compared to this tongue-tied, virtually illiterate peasant, Mikhail Alexeyevich. You know he believes. The strength of his belief is immediately palpable; it merges his fate with the fates of his wife, children, and grandchildren. He believes in goodness, kindness, and the prohibition against people killing animals needlessly or for fun. We drank tea and talked, and his bearing and what he said left me with a fond memory of him.

I traveled from Yerevan to Sassoon village on the slopes of Mount Aragats yesterday for a wedding. Kochar's sister, an old woman, married off her son, who's a driver. This trip was, without a doubt, my most powerful Armenian experience. It wasn't the marvelous, poetic, rough, complex, and multi-layered wedding ceremony with the beautiful ancient songs David Sassoon's[1] village is famous for, but the people, Syoma, the old rural Armenians, the peasants, they're wonderful people.

At the wedding, there were 200 souls, and I, for the first time in my life, heard so many humane speeches. Dozens of people addressed me; in front of a crowd of men and women, they spoke passionately, emotionally, and with tears. Shepherds, drivers,

---

1   *David Sassoon the popular warrior symbol of Armenia's struggle against the Arabs.

sailors, rural masons, they all spoke. I particularly regretted that you weren't there that day in that village. I thought you'd have stood and cried, written a poem, and people would cry reading it.

And all this took place amid rough piles of stones, against a backdrop of blue sky, and the people who wrote the Bible saw the same Mount Ararat's shining peaks. Oh, Syoma, it was so affecting, when I see you, I'll tell you all about it in detail, and maybe you'll see it with your own eyes. It's worth going; you must …

The fact that Munblit limited his edit to names and dates was something of an achievement. And with regards to Valya and Ruvochka[1], I must say my humility ranks so low or so high that their phone calls to you made me happy. And finally, Ruvim himself phoned and spoke to you. But I won't attribute too much to that.

30th December 1961

… Syoma, I'm finished. I'll reckon up with the author, collect my fee and go to Sukhumi, where you can write to me 'on demand.' Obviously, I won't leave 'til the third. I am so tired that other than a nervous breakdown and a wanton desire to cry, I don't feel anything. The conversations with the client are sharp. He's an intelligent man and understands I've done this well, but at the same time, he can't help hating me as though he were an animal caught in the clutches of Dr. Moreau[2], and Dr. Moreau has indeed severely cut and crushed him, and thereby somewhat raised him

---

1   *The Fraermans.
2   +Comparing Grossman to the character in H G Wells' *Dr Moreau's Island* (Heinemann, Stone & Kimball, 1896).

on the ladder of literary evolution. But of course, it hurts, "Where is my wool? Why is my tail cut off? I don't want to be naked and shorn," and at the same time, it's pleasant. You're also an old and experienced Dr. Moreau; admit it, it comes naturally to you![1] You know these situations better than me. Yesterday I finished this back-breaking work, and today began to write a record of my Armenian experience. Like George Sand, at 4AM, I finish a novel and start another without going to bed. However, there's a difference between us; she was published. In my case, it's really quite hard to understand; what's the rush?

I want to see you. Time's passed, there's more and more to talk about, and the pen, as they say, is powerless. It is possible that before I leave, we'll go and see Kochar's relatives in the Ararat Valley. There's nothing like people's lives in Ararat's rich, heavenly valley.

30th December 1961, evening

... I was paid at the publishing house except for my royalties, of course. They'll come once the book's released, just like they do in Moscow. It seems the author decided I'd work faster if I received payment for its circulation once the manuscript was delivered. I find it strange that after living here for 2 months, no writers came to see me or on passing me in the street, even asked after my health or if this was my first time in Armenia?

I've never seen more dogged indifference; it

---

1 *The last few words need clarification. In 1937 at the open party meeting the critic Elena Usievich was picked to pieces. During the break she was approached by poet Michael Golodny who said, "Usyevich, admit it, you're an enemy of the people, it comes naturally to you."

seems hardly possible. It isn't even indifference; it's rudeness because asking an elderly visitor how he is and if he likes a new place is a matter of common decency.

When we last conversed, my author suggested (and very strongly, too) that where the word 'people' appeared in the manuscript, it should be replaced by 'men'. He was surprised I couldn't see his argument that 'men' sounded softer, warmer, more cordial.

Leaving that aside, I've seen Armenia's wonders.

11th January 1962

Dear Syoma,

I am writing to you in this new year from Sukhumi. All the sea is evergreen, and the rain and sun are spring warm ... Before leaving Armenia, or rather, on the day I left, I saw something powerful. We went to the famous Ararat cognac distillery in the morning, diligently tasted the brandy, and then went on to the blessed Ararat valley. In a village there, I found out for myself, with certainty, that I liked country people more than Armenia's churches and mountains. It was so good to sit with them in a rock-built house, to drink grape vodka and talk, to look at the old men's lovely faces ...

I very much look forward to you developing a relationship with *Novy Mir*. I know it will take them a year to publish you, but you can't retract your submission; the years are passing. My new year began like everything in my life does, it was good, happy, sad, anxious, and confused, but I was in good spirits with a desire to work. Life's illogical, as pointless as it is invincible. I'll tell you about that good, happy, difficult, and demanding when we meet, and that won't be in the Armenian mountains.

A harsh letter from O M[1] was forwarded to me from Begovaya. I wrote assuring her that I knew that Katya[2] was in Sochi, that I was going to Sukhumi before coming back to Moscow, but would also go to Sochi to see everyone. Oh, what a bitter mess this is.

I'll be back around the 20th. The sea and palm trees bow to you cordially and not only them ...[3]

Grossman returned to Moscow at the beginning of 1962. The fact that he'd lost weight and was very tanned didn't make him look any younger. He looked sick. Even when he was joking and laughing, there was excruciating pain in his eyes, and I could see it was not physical but mental. He moved to a one-room cooperative flat not far from my home but found living alone dreary. When I comforted him by describing the temptations and charms of bachelorhood, he just smiled weakly and helplessly. A neighbor knocked on his door and told him some electricians had been, and they'd asked whether Grossman really lived next door to him (these 'electricians' were probably installing bugs). Grossman was disinterested in what his neighbors had to say.

His fortitude was great; he worked hard, produced several short stories, and wrote up his notes on Armenia, which I can't help but call a poem. I emphasize that if anyone in Russia reads my memoirs, and if, moreover, they are a writer, I think they'll read Grossman's Armenian letters with interest and then follow up on how they were transformed into a work of art. Grossman's last work is unexpected. He'd never written so frankly about himself. He reveals not only his soul but also his

---

1 *Olga Mikhailovna (Grossman's wife).

2 *Yekaterina Zabolotskaya (Grossman's lover).

3 *The allusion to my poem 'Nestor and Saria', which takes place in Sukhumi (a translation of 'Nestor and Saria' appears in *A Close Reading of 53 Poems by Semyon Izrailevich Lipkin* by Alexander Solzhenistyn, Yvonne Green and Sergei Makarov (Hendon Press, 2023)).

physiology and flesh. He had never been so close to himself and never approached men's faces with such pleasure: "It seemed not to be candles, but people's eyes that shone with a soft, lovely fire."

I beg to hold the reader's attention on one point. After Stalin's death, there was a literary revival. Along with realistic works, without which literature felt suffocated, verses appeared, which were called self-expression, prose poems, and confessional. This may sound strange – are there artists who don't express themselves? And what literary work is not a confession? But the fact is that after the courtly Stalinist literature, which imitated canons inherited from the East's courtly poetry, the reader had every reason to want something new. To be sure, some things from the period of post-Stalin 'confessional expression' bear the mark of talent, but far from all artists starting to express themselves, they found nothing to express. They began to confess, but it turned out that everyone had sinned, and all in the same primitive way. It was then that, as a way to distinguish themselves from one another, they resorted to metaphor and ornamentation, precisely as the Persian poet-courtiers of the Middle Ages did. The same formulae led to the same resolutions. Confession and self-expression are only interesting and deep when the artist is deep and interesting.

Returning to *Dobro Vam*, it contains all that is great, sad, luminous, and powerful in Grossman's earlier books but also something new and striking which isn't so easy to define with a critic's pen. And I'm not trying to express my thoughts about Grossman's Armenian poem here. I think what's more important is to tell the story of the book's publication, which in itself is sad and devoid of light.

When he'd finished, Grossman gave the book to *Novy Mir*. Tvardovsky liked it and only commented once next to the passage, "When you've drunk too much my middle-aged and elderly brothers, surely you know what it's like to wake up in the middle of the night," Tvardovsky's marginal read, "You bet!" There were no other comments, and the essay-poem was typed up. The censor gave the galley its life-giving stamp but suggested – effectively ordered – that one paragraph be cut. The reader will remember the passage from the letter of December 25, where Grossman wrote:

> This trip was, without a doubt, my most powerful Armenian experience ... for the first time in my life, I heard so many kind, humane speeches.

The following are the lines that created the strongest impression in the book and frightened the censors:

> I bow to the Armenian peasants who, in a mountain village, amid wedding revels, publicly spoke of the pain of the Jewish people during Hitler's terror, about the death camps where the German Nazis murdered Jewish women and children. I bow down to everyone who solemnly, sadly, in silence, listened to these speeches. Their faces and eyes said a lot to me. I bow to the sad words about those killed in clay ditches, gas, and earth pits, to the sad words about the living, in whose eyes are framed the words of hate and contempt. 'It's a pity Hitler didn't finish you all off.'
> Until the end of my life, I'll remember the peasants' speeches I heard in that country.

The censor's decision offended and enraged Grossman. At his insistence, Tvardovsky tried to persuade his journal's censor but was unsuccessful. In these lines, the ever-vigilant censor perceived a slight to the state, and their suppression was inexorable. Grossman refused to print *Dobro Vam* in *Novy Mir*.

I understood him. His signature on that letter to Stalin haunted him; he didn't want to compromise his honor again. After the arrest of *Life and Fate*, it hurt him to make concessions, to sacrifice his memoirs like this. I wasn't one of those writer-slaves to whom Grossman's intransigence seemed foolish or the manifestation of a cantankerous nature, but I still think that Grossman made a mistake. Of course, the 10 or 12 lines *Novy Mir* had ringed with prohibitive red pencil were very dear to Grossman, but *Dobro Vam* was about a hundred pages long, and what priceless thoughts readers would have found there, what deep sentiments would have come to them.

Grossman's Armenian notes became known in literary circles. The galleys were read. This is what the writer Frieda Vigdorova, a woman who felt things very deeply, wrote to Grossman, "I've read *Dobro Vam*. It's as beautiful as it could be. Bitter, tender, piercing. You're a wonderful writer, and these hundred pages belong among your best work. One sees everybody you do, thinks along with you, cries, and laughs. It's such a joy to read, though not easy."

After Grossman's death, the Armenian poet Silva Kaputikyan[1] happened to read the galley of *Dobro Vam*. These notes spoke to the patriot in her, and she took the manuscript Grossman had dedicated to her people and tried to get it published at home. Except for a few lines, the essay had received the stamp of Moscow's censor, which was treated with, quite naturally, full authority in Armenia. Nothing was heard about its publication for about a year. After Grossman's death, I went to Armenia, as I'd promised him I would, and it turned out that the galley was with the Russian language magazine *Literaturnaya Armenia* [*Literary Armenia*]. Because of the section red-lined by the censor, the editors of *Literaturnaya Armenia* were afraid to publish it at all, although they very much wanted to. With the help of my friend, Levon Mkrtchyan, a professor of literature, I managed to convince them they'd be safe if they published and how important it was that they did. *Dobro Vam* was already being talked about in Yerevan. In 1965, *Literaturnaya Armenia* finally published it, naturally excluding the prohibited paragraph. I understand that I went against

---

1 +Silva Kaputikyan (1919–2006), leading Armenian poet and activist.

Grossman's wishes, but I think I did the right thing by pressing for the publication on terms that differed from Grossman's. Such wonderful work should not be inaccessible to readers.[1]

My visit to Yerevan coincided with the fiftieth anniversary of the genocide when the Turks slaughtered a million Armenians. The press didn't mention this terrible event. The Russian newspapers carried an editorial on the success of how fields were being plowed in conformity, and the Armenian newspaper spoke of the friendship between the Soviet Union's peoples.[2] There was unrest in the city. It began in the morning. The massive crowd in the square in front of the Spendiarov Theatre didn't want to disperse. Young people were asking that the area of Karabakh populated by Armenians be detached from the territory of Azerbaijan. I saw something symbolic in the fact that our negotiations with the editors about Grossman's notes on Armenia were conducted to the distant roar of an ever-growing, incessantly angry crowd.

When *Literaturnaya Armenia* appeared in Moscow, a long-term friend of Grossman, a *Novy Mir* employee Anna Berzer, advised me to go to Tvardovsky with a proposal to reprint *Dobro Vam* in its section, 'Pages From Other Magazines' (which republished small pieces from provincial journals). Tvardovsky sat with me on the Commission on Grossman's literary legacy, and my duty, among other things, was to report to him about its meetings when he didn't attend. Berzer advised me to approach Tvardovsky to talk the authorities into transferring the manuscript of *Life and Fate* from the Lubyanka (KGB) to the closed archive of TsGALI[3], which was far more accessible

---

1   +Lipkin's recollection is inaccurate in that *Literaturnaya Armenia* didn't omit this passage although they accepted a few other cuts suggested by Moscow. Lipkin neither mentions those cuts or their adoption by *Literaturnaya Armenia*.

2   +Natalie Gonchar-Khanjyan counters this assertion in *Literaturnaya Armenia*, 1989, No. 2, pp76-87 [Н.А.Гончар-Ханджян // Литературная Армения. 1989. - № 2. - c. 76-87], and claims that the events described by the autho° were covered in the Armenian press at the time.

3   +Central Archives for Art and Literature.

to the Commission's members. Tvardovsky promised to help in respect of the latter, but he said he did not want to be rushed. For an approach to succeed, he'd have to choose the right time to raise it with one of the state's leaders.

When I passed on the request with respect to publication, Tvardovsky was blunt and said he refused to reprint *Dobro Vam*. He said he admired Vasily's moral fortitude but considered his writing mediocre. I reminded him of how he used to laud Grossman and had even been enthusiastic. Tvardovsky began to swear and curse, and I swore and cursed back. Only Yuz Aleshkovsky could have written what formed the substance of that literary exchange.[1] The history of *Dobro Vam* didn't end there; our heritage committee managed to publish it in a slim collection of short stories Grossman had written over various years. It was published by Sovetsky Pisatel' [Soviet Writers] in 1967; they gave it the title of the first story he'd written after *Life and Fate* was arrested. The collections' editor, Vera Ostrogorskaya, a good woman, told me that the editorial board was ruthless and cut not just lines but entire pages and chapters of Grossman's manuscript. I want to emphasize that these weren't the actions of Glavlit (the Chief Censor's Office) but of the editorial board comprised of writers.

I passed on what Vera Ostrogorskaya had told me at a meeting of our heritage committee. Its members decided not to raise objections with Sovetsky Pisatel'. At first, I wanted to persuade the Committee to refuse to publish a distorted version of *Dobro Vam*. However, after much thought, I decided not to do so, first, for the reasons stated above, that bringing it to readers was important, and secondly, because it was unlikely I would have successfully prevailed over the Committee.

Now I feel both joy that Russian readers had access to most of *Dobro Vam* and guilt in respect of my friend whose wishes I failed to uphold after his death.

---

1   +Iosif Aleshkovsky, known as Yuz Aleshkovsky (born 1929), is a contemporary author notorious for swearing in Russian.

Here's an extract from what became chapter two at the book's publication but was originally the third chapter of Grossman's manuscript. The second was cut entirely:

On the mountain over Yerevan, there's a monument to Stalin. Whatever your vantage point, you can see the gigantic bronze Marshal. He wears a long bronze overcoat, a military cap on his head, and his bronze hand lays beneath his overcoat's lapel. He strides, his step slow, heavy, and calm; he's in no hurry. This giant projects a strange and conflicting combination of powers, at once so vast only a god could possess them, yet, at the same time, brutal and earthly, military and bureaucratic. It seems as though the clouds touch Stalin's head. He's seventeen meters tall and stands fifty-two meters high on his pedestal. When the monument was being erected, and parts of its vast bronze body lay on the ground, the workers building it could stand and walk through Stalin's hollow legs unbowed.

I arrived in Yerevan during the Twenty-Second Party Congress when Stalin Avenue, that wide, straight, plane tree-lined, lamp-posted, most beautiful street, was being renamed Lenin Avenue. My Armenian acquaintances spoke with dignity when they said, "Let the metal that went into the creation of this monument regain the original nobility of its nature ...."

I was told that at a general meeting of the collective farmers in one village in the Ararat valley, the suggestion was made to remove the monument to Stalin. The peasants said, "The state collected a hundred thousand rubles to erect it. Please destroy it, but give our money back to us."

It seemed that only old Andreas[1] (crazed by the mass killings of Armenians) was upset when Stalin's monument was removed. He shook his staff, threw himself at the driver, children, and students who'd come up from Yerevan to ski. For him, Stalin beat the Germans. And the Germans were the Turks' allies. To him, Stalin's monument had been destroyed by Turkish agents.

When *Dobro Vam* was published, four pages were removed from Grossman's fifth chapter (the book's fourth). They included a story about an old man called Sarkisyan, a great party leader in his youth, who'd met Lenin in exile. He was arrested as a Turkish spy, badly beaten, and sent to a Siberian camp where he lived for nineteen years. Grossman recounts that:

He told me how there were eighty highly educated people from Yerevan imprisoned in one narrow cell – professors, former revolutionaries, sculptors, architects, artists, well-known doctors – and what a painfully long time it took for the guards, who kept losing count, to keep tally of them. Then one day, they came into the cell with a sullen old man who glanced at the crammed bunks and floor and left immediately. He did the same every day thereafter. It later transpired he was a shepherd and that the administration had deployed his phenomenal skill in keeping a tally of his sheep, whether they numbered hundreds or thousands, to keep a record of their flock of prisoners.

He told me that when he came back from camp, he started selling soda water on Yerevan's Abovyan Street, and one old peasant had a long conversation

---

1   +Grossman's 'Madman of Tsakhazdor', who conflates the two world wars.

with him while he drank his water. Sarkisyan told him that he had been involved in underground work, helped overthrow the Tsar in 1917 and build the Soviet regime, been sent to the camp, and now sold soda. The old peasant had thought for a moment and then asked, 'Why did you overthrow the Tsar? Did he stop you from selling soda water?'

There followed a touching story about how two large Russian Molokan families had recently waded across the Arak river at night from Turkey to Armenia. The commander of the border outpost greeted them cordially, and the wives of the border officers ran forward with clothes for the women and children. I don't understand why this episode was cut by the editors. The Molokans ran toward, not away from us; the story flattered us.

The foreword to the book was written by Nikolai Atarov. It was quite good; he was perceptive. He wrote of Grossman:

> In life, he was as reserved, disinterested in the superficial, and menacing as justice itself … It's only now, rereading his posthumous collection of short stories, you realize how this reclusive man tirelessly searched the roads and trails to the people, and how this author, who sometimes offended those who loved him, hated it when friendship was betrayed.

That's accurate: Grossman was uncomfortable with superficial friendships and hated betrayal. But how can you call something friendship if it's superficial? Does an acquaintance made at a party at the Writer's House always turn into a friendship? Grossman demanded honesty, perseverance, and self-denial from his friends. A reasonable expectation in a reasonable society. Grossman wanted his friends to be "straight and devoid of hypocrisy."

Grossman's problem was that he could be gullible, and

this gullibility was aggravated by one weakness: he welcomed admirers. He acquired friends easily; during the war, he was honored and fêted at a time when all kinds of people were thrown together and shared sorrows and hardships. But when these military hardships were replaced by those of another sort, people changed and reverted to type. Atarov had clung to Grossman, used to visit him like a student visits his teacher, and Grossman welcomed him, but after Atarov became a party worker, he was appointed editor of the magazine *Moskva* [*Moscow*], and he gradually distanced himself from the now-persecuted Grossman. It would hardly be a surprise if Grossman did look "grim and menacing" when they ran into each other.

The war had brought Grossman and Boris Galin together. This *Pravda* essayist was proud to be close to Grossman, and Grossman, was flattered by his adulation; I could see that. However, Galin faded away when Grossman was in trouble. And if Grossman had known how despicably Galin would behave after his death when *Everything Flows* was published abroad, he would, no doubt, have been "grim and menacing" to him too.

Grossman had a childhood friend who became a professor of mathematics. During the "struggle against cosmopolitanism," he said, "In the name of the idea of communism, it is permissible to sacrifice an entire people." The professor had children late in his life whom he adored like all fathers, yet he said, "In the name of communism, I am ready to sacrifice my own children." Was that a slave's hypocrisy or stupidity? Maybe the professor also wondered why Grossman seemed "grim and menacing."

Grossman liked the critic Fyodor Levin (I venture to suggest that this was because he admired Grossman's oeuvre). He showed empathy when Levin was slanderously denounced by his fellow soldier and friend, the poet Kovalenkov. Levin was tried and convicted on the Northern Front of recklessly candid speech. However, when Yermilov fulminated in *Pravda* against Grossman's play, *According to the Pythagoreans*, the same Fyodor Levin said, "If I'd written this review, I'd have done so more gently." After reading those words from Levin, was it any wonder that Grossman became "grim and menacing"?

Grossman had a friend and literary fan called Osip Chernyi[1]. Grossman both liked him as a fan and admired his knowledge of music. Grossman both loved and wanted to expand his knowledge of music. Chernyi once called Grossman "A lucky, spoilt child" when contrasting his own literary fortunes to Grossman's. Grossman didn't react at the time but told me about it later, which meant it had stuck in his mind and offended him. Chernyi later produced a novel about the musicians Stalin attacked as "formalists," alleging they "created confusion instead of music." The characters in Chernyi's novel were thinly veiled versions of Shostakovich, Myaskovsky, and Prokofiev. These composers weren't close to Grossman's heart, but he preferred them to Mozart or Beethoven. Chernyi's attack angered Grossman, whose attitude to him became "grim and menacing."

I don't remember who told me that the journalist Ardamatsky was in Koktebel at the same time as Grossman. Ardamatsky had written the acclaimed but antisemitic essay, 'Pinya from Zhmerinka', published in the humorous magazine *Krokodil* [*Crocodile*]. None of the decent writers spoke to Ardamatsky after its publication, but Grossman did. He bewildered those good writers by saying, "I don't see how Ardamatsky is any worse than the others, so do you think I should stop saying hello to everyone?" Naturally, anyone hearing these words was cut to the quick.

I myself once became a victim of Grossman's intransigence. It was in 1948 when, at a meeting on the problems of translation, the poet and translator Lev Penkovsky spoke against

---

1   +Osip Evseevich Chernyi (1899-1981), Russian Soviet writer.

Pasternak. Aseyev[1], Grossman's partner at cards, who'd been at the meeting, told him that it had been me who'd spoken out against Pasternak. Aseyev had obviously confused me with Penkovsky because we'd both translated Kyrgyz epics. I was told that Grossman raged and cursed at me, and I stopped seeing him. It took several months until we met at a ceremony where we were both awarded medals on the occasion of Moscow's 800th anniversary. Grossman came up to me and smiled. It turned out he'd learned of his mistake from Nikolai Chukovsky. We kissed, were reconciled, and I said, "You should have asked me what had happened." Grossman said guiltily, "I believed the worst; you always do at times like that."

Grossman liked Ehrenburg and found his attitude attentive, affectionate and respectful. Grossman appreciated his talent, which showed especially clearly in his view of Ehrenburg's novel *Julio Jurenito*. He valued his military articles, education, and excellent knowledge of painting and was glad of the praise of a senior writer who was world-famous.

Grossman shrugged when I said that Ehrenburg was a true, though minor poet, a reasonable translator, a mediocre novelist, and an unscrupulous journalist given to hyperbole. My opinion seemed to Vasily to be an unsubstantiated paradox, except with regard to his journalistic hyperbole. One day, sometime in the early fifties, Grossman and I were visiting Kaverin[2] and spent the night at his country house in Peredelkino. Ehrenburg, who lived nearby in a dacha with Lidin[3], heard we were there and invited us over. Grossman was irritated; he'd been drinking vodka, which had been generously offered. So when we arrived at Lidin's, Grossman attacked Ehrenburg's political activity and called him an appeaser. Ehrenburg was stoic as he listened quietly to Grossman's offensive.

---

1   +Nikolai Aseyev (1889-1963), well known Russian poet.
2   +Veniamin Kaverin (1902-1989), Soviet author best known for *The Two Captains*.
3   +VladImir Lidin (1894-1979), prolific Soviet author.

I agreed with Grossman but disapproved of his behavior. He had fallen out with so many people and was now falling out with Ehrenburg, who loved him as a writer and a person. Because our society was unique, unusual, and new, it was difficult – sometimes impossible – to interact with people in the way we had in the old one, which, although imperfect, had seemed normal to us.

No, Grossman was not "grim and menacing", but he became that way. He loved celebrating, having fun, having friendly chats, joking, and playing poker or whist (sometimes around the clock for days on end). He was open to people, heart and soul, and believed in people to the point of gullibility, but once he was repeatedly and roughly deceived, he became suspicious. And those who had deceived and betrayed him called him menacing, moody, and reclusive to avoid culpability.

On December 12th, 1984, he would have been 79. Most of his peers are dead now. Just a few of the writers who knew him remain in Moscow. When Life and Fate was published, interest in him revived. Those lucky ones who managed to read it were enthralled by it. They came to see me to discuss it and its author, and I kept hearing, "He was a hard, unsociable, angry man." I reminded them how he was shunned in his gravest hour and by whom. Since I expressed my attitude without anger, with a smile (because I had no respect for those people), they didn't take offense. Grossman's mistake, in my opinion, was that he took the new type of literary people too seriously and tried to judge them by the old standards of Russia's intelligentsia.

In late 1962, Grossman told me that doctors had found blood in his urine. The Literary Fund clinic's attending physician, Dr. Raysky, advised him to apply to the urologist but didn't press him. Grossman didn't do so.

We both thought this blood could have been caused by the highly spiced food he'd so enjoyed in Armenia. The unpleasant symptoms abated, and Grossman felt relieved. The oncologists told me later that if he'd been treated earlier, he'd have been saved or at least have prolonged his life by five or six years. Grossman seemed to forget the incident and worked hard and animatedly but kept complaining about his health, which was unusual for him. He read newspapers daily, listened to critics on the radio[1], and watched his friends' literary progress with compassion and love. This is what he wrote to me when I was in Maleyevka:

Dear Syoma,

I received your letter. I'm glad you're feeling better. Glad your last poem was finally published in *Literaturnaya Gazeta*.

Are you surprised? Because before you left, you told me that the editors had decided not to publish any of these poems. Anyway, I'm delighted that this is the ninth of your poems to be published. I'm glad that you 'walk alone' and say, 'with such a companion, I can never get bored.'

How heavy such a companion can be. Remember how painful it can be to communicate with him sometimes. '… And reading … despite the life, I had before, / I curse the world, and tremble, breathless, / And bitterly complain, and shed my tears sore ….'[2]

Oh, this man with whom we never get bored; he is reciprocal, all depends on how you treat him. I have absolutely no news, 'Out upon the highway / Hushed and empty all, / Now the howling watch-dogs / Even, silent fall.'[3]

By the way, Katya[4] told me that Dickens (she's now translating his letters) separated from his wife

---

1   +Refers to the Western media.
2   +Alexander Pushkin 's 'Remembrance', 1928 (trans. Yevgeny Bonver).
3   +Ivan Nikitin's 'Winter Night In The Village' 1853. (Martha Gilbert Dickinson Bianchi Trans).
4   +Grossman's daughter.

when they had 10 children. I'm writing this with no fear of arousing dangerous thoughts in anyone on this occasion because I know that only bad examples are contagious …

And this comes from his letter of February 4th 1963:

… I am delighted with Dorofeyev's little article about you.[1] I've read it several times. One can hardly write better. I keep remembering how you used to say, "If at least 5 lines are published in 30 years …."

Well, finally, here they are. I think they'll help a lot in the business of publishing, although, of course, you shouldn't be too optimistic. They, however, bear something more than their practical application, they're good and important in themselves. They're important in the first place not only for those who read them but for you too. And that's why I was happy reading and rereading them. Incidentally, I thought that *Literaturnaya Gazeta* could have published an excerpt from the long poem[2], too, even if they won't take it all … Gecht feels better, his temperature has dropped, and the doctors are optimistic. He's begun to show an interest in the outside world and asked for newspapers. But the danger persists.[3]

I have nothing new; those who were silent remain silent ….

---

1   *I have read for the first time in my life an article in the *Literaturnaya Gazetta* about a joint meeting which I organized of the Poets and Translators' Union.

2   +'The Technical Lieutenant-Quartermaster', recently translated and reprinted in *A Close Reading of 53 poems by Semyon Izrailevich Lipkin* (Hendon Press, 2023).

3   *Semyon Gecht, our friend who I mentioned previously, had been operated on for a benign tumour, but eight years in camp had weakened his health, he was very feeble and died in hospital shortly after the operation.

13th February 1963

... I am glad there's progress with 'Nestor'[1] in *Literaturnaya Rossiya*[2]. But, of course, many, many obstacles still lie ahead. How are things with the collection? You didn't tell me what Slutsky[3] said about its horoscope. Why don't you write about who's in Maleyevka? I'm always curious to read your lists and comments.

I don't write about my business because nothing significant, either positive or negative, has happened. Anna Samoilovna called once and said vaguely that she can't take the story for now, that I must wait. I was slightly surprised when she said she'd read it considering the editorial situation.

Berezko[4] shows no signs of life. I don't feel very well; my blood pressure's jumped up again. Yesterday I saw Raysky, but I, Don Pomerantz[5], keep writing and writing.

21st February 1963

... Katya[6] arrived from Leningrad yesterday. Things are terrible there; her sister's husband had cancer, the

---

1   *[Lipkin's] poem, 'Nestor and Saria.' *Literary Russia* was going to publish it, but after Khrushchev's speech at the exhibition in Manezh they rejected it categorically. The poem was eventually first published in the magazine, *Time and Us* which is available in Israel. Also translated by Yvonne Green and Sergei Makarov in *A Close Reading of 53 Poems by Semyon Izrailevich Lipkin* (Hendon Press, 2023).

2   +The weekly newspaper of the RSFSR, The Writers' Union.

3   *The poet Boris Slutsky decided to collect my poems for *The Soviet Writer*. This is how my first book *Ochevidets* [*Eyewitness*] 1967 was published.

4   *Georgy Berezko, writer and later chairman of the committee for Grossman's Literary Legacy.

5   +Reference to a humorous poem popular at the turn of the century.

6   *Ekaterina Zabolotskaya.

doctors refuse to operate as they believe it won't help, and he's been discharged from the hospital. Imagine, he himself is an oncological surgeon and didn't know he had cancer. It's always so sad when people get old; they feel the world's full of hypertension, multiple sclerosis, malignant tumors, and tachycardia. When we were twenty, it felt like there was nothing worse in the world than venereal disease.

There's no chance Anna Samoilovna will take my story; this type of thing's destined to be read by 'Editors Only.'

Write to me when you're coming back. You're rolling around like a Danish cheese in Vologda butter amid astronomers and Sokolov-Mikitovs ...[1]

In April, Grossman's bad symptoms recurred. The doctors decided to send him to hospital. He was admitted to a double room at Botkin Hospital on the eve of May Day. Marinin, Pravda's political columnist, was in the bed next to him. He hadn't been close to Grossman, but he did distract him with interesting snippets of information. Grossman's operation was going to be performed by an experienced surgeon, the urologist Dr. Gudynsky, who told us that the disease, cancer of the kidney, had been neglected, that he would remove the kidney, but wasn't sure that there was no metastasis. Grossman didn't pass water before the surgery. We sat on a bench in the hospital garden every day, where he was quiet and reconciled. Only patients' rudeness, vacuous conversations, and manners at meals annoyed Grossman. He no longer saw 'ordinary' people like he used to, "with overarching love."

We told him he had nephritis, an unpleasant but not

---

1   +Ivan Sergeevich Sokolov-Mikitov (1882-1975) was a Russian/Soviet writer and journalist who took part in numerous journeys and expeditions. His most famous trip was the one Otto Schmidt led to the Arctic Circle in the icebreaker 'Georgy Sedov' in 1929-30.

dangerous condition, that his kidney wasn't working and had to be removed. He listened warily but believed us. At least, it seemed to me that he did. Olga, Ekaterina Zabolotskaya, his daughter Katya, and the writer Alexander Pismenny all visited him. Once Galina, his first wife, came from Kharkiv to Moscow. He was displeased.

The operation went well. Gudynsky said, "It might turn out alright." A few days later, I had to fly urgently for two weeks to Dushanbe. I arranged with Ekaterina Zabolotskaya that she would write to me in detail.

Here is her letter of 11th May 1963:

> ...Vasily was allowed to get up, take a few steps and sit in a chair. And today, he took a bath. He says that he experienced bliss, though he was afraid at first. In the evening, in my presence, he demonstrated all of his achievements, walked to the window, and had supper sitting in a chair. He moved slowly, with difficulty, but without support. It was apparent he'd lost weight, and his skin color was bad.
>
> On 9th May three ladies visited him, Anna Samoilovna, Maryam Naumovna[1], and Hasmik. I'm told they discussed editorial news very noisily and tired him out. On the 10th, Vasya's wound had not been re-dressed for a long time, and the bandage was in poor condition.
>
> He says that from the doctors' faces, he can see that they don't think his wound looks good. It's still weeping. They say that now that he can sit up and walk a bit, his blood circulation will get better, which will improve everything.
>
> Objectively it looks better, but he gets sadder and more dispirited. Today, the first time since the operation, when he walked to the window, he said,

---

1   *Maryam Chernevich, a French to Russian translator.

"I've come to breathe and look out at the windows of The Cancer Institute."[1]

Vasya asks me to convey his warm greetings. We were going to write to you together, but today he was so tired from his travels that he couldn't even dictate a few phrases ...

From Ekaterina Zabolotskaya, 16th May 1963:

Dear Syoma,

I've become a grandmother, my granddaughter was born yesterday at 10.50 ...

Vasya is good and I think he's getting better. He goes outside. They take him up and down by elevator and he walks alone without support. I found him sitting on a bench in the street. His mood was better, although he says nothing makes him happy, neither spring nor greenery which he wanted to see so much ...

After being discharged from hospital, Grossman got noticeably stronger, and his complexion improved. One would have been glad had one not been aware of the impending threat. Every day we walked together near the house, sometimes urged on by the momentum inherent in both of us. We took a tram, rode its long route from start to finish, and watched passengers change. If we saw children holding their mothers' hands, Grossman would make faces at them, and the children would laugh. Sometimes we went by taxi to the river port, sat in the park, and admired the river and steamers. With tears in his voice, he told me that a young writer Ovidy Gorchakov[2] had come to Gudynsky and offered Grossman his kidney.

In August, he read me the final version of his novel,

---

1   *The Cancer Institute, named by Pyotr Herzen, is located next door to the Botkin Hospital.

2   +Ovidy Gorchakov (1924-2000), Soviet writer and spy.

Everything Flows, which he'd worked on all those months since he'd left hospital. To me, *Everything Flows* is a milestone in Russian prose – its lacunae are apparent, and its relationship to feature page journalism results from a deliberate decision by Grossman and doesn't denote hasty composition, as some assert.

In this story, Grossman deals with things never touched on by any writer before him. I've never seen it in published form, but the main characters are based on people who are well-known to me.[1]

In Autumn, The Literary Fund sent Grossman to a military sanatorium at Arkhangelskoye near Moscow. He wrote to me from there on 11th September 1963:

> Hello, dear Syoma!
>
> I'm writing to you from the sanatorium in Arkhangelskoye, sitting in a separate room, not a hallway. The sanatorium's plush and surrounded by nature. It is all so beautiful, the old park with huge trees, under which the Moscow River flows fast. The fine facilities here include movies, billiards, and the dining room in particular. The place has the kind of military feel with which I've lost touch since Autumn 1945. On the first day, I did a lot of walking. The classical marble sculptures are especially beautiful against the lawns in which they're set. Antokolsky's figure of the dead 22-year-old Yusupova is lovely. Pavel lags a long way behind his uncle ... I left Moscow in a heavy, lousy mood ...

From a letter dated 16th September 1963:

> ... I called you twice on Friday (you can't call me here), but you didn't pick up the phone ... The

---

1 +*Everythng Flows* was published in the West in 1973.

weather, unfortunately, gets worse from day to day. I'm a little troubled by asthma, probably because of the moisture and greenery, but it's not terrible, and there are many doctors and the medicine's good here … Every night I go to the movies, I still haven't met anyone we know. Yablochkina's resting here. We don't have fun – I don't make love to her. I called Anna Samoilovna; apparently, they've buried me in *Nedelya* [*The Week*].

Grossman's last letter to me was dated 6th October 1963:

… I feel better and stronger; my asthma's troubled me less recently, and I've lost 5 pounds. In 2 or 3 days, I'll go back to Gudynsky. I'm unaccustomed to hospital, and it scares me …

But he only went to hospital at the beginning of the winter rather than immediately after he left the sanatorium. He had become very sick, and it was evident that he was dying. The causes of cancer are so unresearched, but one that can't be ruled out is severe nervous shock. I've no doubt he got ill because *Life and Fate* was arrested; otherwise, he could have lived a long time. His father had died in his eighties. But Grossman was thrown away in the prime of his life, cast out of the literary process. On the eve of the war, the same fate befell Mikhail Bulgakov, another leading light of Russian literature. The medical records are different, but the disease is the same. Remember that Bulgakov had his *Dog's Heart* arrested.

When Grossman returned to Botkin Hospital, he had a room to himself. It was narrow and long, like a coffin. A decision was made not to operate; he had lung cancer. The doctors thought it was senseless to keep him in hospital, and one of them said, "Let him die at home."

Dreary months followed. Grossman tried to work and read; he became morose and irritable and didn't believe our deception that he'd recover. We learned of a drug in Baku, extracted from crude oil, which cured lung cancer. We managed to get it through Imran Gasimov, the head of Azerbaijan's writers. Grossman took it under the supervision of a doctor, but he didn't improve. There was talk about another drug from France, also alleged to be miraculous. It turned out that Lilya Brik was taking it. She'd heard that Grossman, like her, took this foreign cure which didn't help. The Litford Clinic's Professor and consultant suggested Grossman have a course of chemotherapy with an experimental drug invented by Professor Emanuel.

The chemotherapy building was a single-storied wooden house behind the first City Hospital. Grossman was given a partitioned private room where his neighbour, the poet Mikhail Svetlov[1], was also dying of cancer. Svetlov was visited by dozens of people every day, it was summer, and many of them queued outside the building. Grossman was always visited by the same few people. He lay on his high bed and listened to his visitors who tried to distract him with all sorts of news. Only one question lit up his eyes, "Will I live?" He wanted to live; he again started to believe our ruse that the doctors had said the prognosis was good.

Once, when I was alone with him, he showed me a small pill and said with a hopeless smile, "Tell me, can this tiny thing save a man?" Then I took out of my pocket a small bottle full of nitroglycerin, poured a pill out onto my palm and said, "Look, this is even smaller, and it saves me." I felt that I should, at least for a moment, console Grossman and convince him of the benefits of treatment because he wanted to be convinced. He wanted to live.

Trouble never comes uncompanioned. At the same time this was happening, my mother got cancer. She was put in Yauzskaya hospital on the Yaroslavl railway line. I had to

---

1   +Mikhail Svetlov (1903-1964), Russian Jewish poet.

travel the distance from one hospital to another. Grossman asked about my mother but was indifferent. In a sense, the outside world was separating from him. On 7th August, we buried my mother at the Vostryakovskoye Cemetery. Ekaterina Zabolotskaya was struck by the severity of the deceased's Jewish ritual bath (men don't attend). She told Grossman this; he listened attentively but was thinking of his own. He died on the night of 15th September 1964.

Soon trouble over the funeral began. Dead writers are ranked in six different ways. First and highest ranked meet their farewells from entire delegations in The Hall of Columns, which was how Fadeyev was buried. Sixth and lowest ranked lie at home in their coffins (in the way Pasternak was buried at Peredelkino), or worse, still in hospital (in the way that Anna Akhmatova lay in the Sklifosovsky Hospital's morgue while speeches were made). Grossman's memorial service, like Platonov's, was ranked fifth. It took place in one of the large rooms at the Writers' Union, but even this had to be pleaded for. The Union determines not only the circumstances of a writer's life but also the procedures governing its members' deaths: will it be announced in *Vechernyaya Moskva* [*Evening Moscow*], will an obituary be placed in *Literaturnaya Gazeta*. Of what size? In what tone? With or without a portrait? With an article by a prominent writer under the obituary, or without one? Who speaks at the funeral? In what cemetery does the burial occur (sometimes more prestigious)? For example, in the German cemetery, they're now only burying writers who spent 50 years in the ranks of the Communist Party. Everything's carefully discussed, and, in special cases, higher authorities are consulted.

Of course, all such matters are in vain, and to the lifeless body, it's all one where it decays.[1] However, man's constitution is such that the living need decorum to ease the pain of loss.

---

1   +A reference to 'Whether I wander...' by Alexander Pushkin.

Arranging things fell to me. The Writers' Union is a ministry; access to those who make decisions isn't simple. I appealed to Nikolai Chukovsky for help; he, by that time, had climbed high up the bureaucratic ladder. He immediately agreed to take me to Tevekelian. I don't now remember who Tevekelian was, whether one of the Moscow writers' organization's secretaries or its main party boss. In contrast to a Russian in the same situation, being an Eastern man, he could remain friendly and cordial. I was well acquainted with Eastern manners.

From my former comrade's first words to Tevekelian, I realized that Nikolai would be of little use. He said, "You see, for a while, I hadn't seen Vasily; we'd had a falling out." Tevekelian noted approvingly, "Yes, yes, I understand you."

I submitted a list of writers who had consented to speak at the memorial service: Ehrenburg, Paustovsky, and Kaverin. "And you?" Tevekelian asked Chukovsky, who refused. Tevekelian didn't insist. After recording those three names, he said, "We'll consider this. If any other issues arise, refer to Voronkov, I'll call right now and tell him to expect you."

Voronkov was the managing secretary of the board of the so-called 'Big Union.' I went to see him alone; Nikolai told me I didn't need him anymore. He was right. Voronkov was important (or rather self-important) and reserved, but I knew that Tevekelian's affability was the mirror of Voronkov's dryness. I put the obituary compiled by Ehrenburg and me on the desk, and Voronkov said, "Leave it; we'll edit it and send it to *Literaturnaya Gazeta*. I asked, "Does Ehrenburg need editing in this case?" "Particularly him," Voronkov interrupted and smiled good-naturedly. And again, I realized that all of these party workers, in effect, are serf actors, each playing a role to appease the lord. If they didn't, they'd be sent under the yoke of serfdom or to the farmyard themselves. I understood that one should seek for human features under these Goldoni masks.

The next day I got an early call from Tevekelian. He said

the memorial service could be held in the conference hall of the Writers' Union and that Evgeny Vorobiev, Ehrenburg, and Alexander Beck could have the floor there. I could speak at the crematorium if I wrote my speech and showed it to him in advance. He told me that the edited obituary had already been sent to *Literaturnaya Gazeta* and *Sovetskaya Kultura* and that I had to bring him a picture of Grossman together with my speech as soon as possible. The decision as to which cemetery could be made later, that there was no hurry since Grossman was being cremated. I asked if everybody had to bring copies of their speeches. Tevekelian didn't answer but said, "I'll expect you at twelve."

I sketched out the text of my speech, got a photograph of Grossman from Olga Mikhailovna, and went back to Tevekelian at the appointed hour. Tevekelian wasn't there, but his secretary said she knew about the case and that I should leave her the photo. She didn't say a single word about leaving my speech.

Around one hundred people came to the civil funeral. They were mostly writers, their wives, and a few readers. Evgeny Vorobyov (whose books I didn't know) spoke warmly, excitedly. I felt that he loved and respected Grossman. Ehrenburg made a clever and serious speech, putting Grossman on a par with Russia's greatest writers. He frankly admitted that Grossman had, in recent years, treated him very critically and stopped seeing him. Ehrenburg said, "The obituary says that the best works of Grossman will remain the common property of the Soviet reader. But who will take it upon themselves to determine what work is the best?"

Everyone understood what he meant. The talented Alexander Beck's speech made an unpleasant impression on me and others of Grossman's friends. He wriggled and winked at everyone as if to say, "Look, I'm wriggling." He wanted to say what he thought of Grossman, that he thought highly of him and felt afraid at the same time. He seemed to be trying to whitewash Grossman in the eyes of invisible authorities, forgetting that the dead no longer needed whitewashing. The literary administration was represented by Tevekelian alone, who also came to the crematorium. We traveled on two buses, and he came in his own car.

At the crematorium, I read my speech as I was told from the page on which I'd written it. Among other things, I said, "We, Grossman's readers, believe that all his works will soon be collected, both the published and the unpublished."

When I said this, there was dead silence; Tevekelian left the crematorium's hall.

Grossman's relatives, Ekaterina Zabolotskaya and I wanted to bury the urn with his ashes at Vagankovskoye Cemetery, next to his father's grave, close to Begovaya street not far from the center of Moscow, where Grossman had lived for many years. But Olga insisted firmly that it be done at Novodevichy, the country's most prestigious cemetery where Mikhail Svetlov, who died about the same time as Grossman, had been buried. Olga wanted the same fate for her husband's remains. The Writers' Union refused to apply for Novodevichy; they said they weren't permitted to do so.

In Moscow, the deputy chairman of the Supreme Soviet of the RSFSR was a Kabardian poet, Alim Keshokov, whose poems I had translated. In the years to come, as head of the Literary Fund, he excluded my wife, the poet Inna Lisnyanskaya and me from this extremely useful organization, but we were on good terms at the time of Grossman's death. With his high-level support, we secured permission to bury the urn containing Grossman's ashes at the Troyekurov graveyard behind Kuntsevo (it suited its name, it was green), which had been founded as an extension to Novodevichy. There is now a granite bust of Grossman at the grave by the sculptor Pismenny (the writer's son).

Grossman rests flanked by Svetlov (a Gypsy writer, not Michael) and the mother of the former Interior Minister, Tikunov. It's hard to get access to Troyekurov; the bus from

Kuntsevo to the subway station is infrequent and irregular. In recent years a decision was made to preserve the cemetery, so no one's buried there anymore. It's a silent town of the dead, rarely visited by the living. Readers don't know where Grossman rests.

It was decided by the Moscow branch of the Writers' Union that the Commission on the literary heritage of Grossman include Georgy Berezko (as chairman), Tvardovsky, Boris Galin, Alexander Pismenny, Miralda Kozlova (from TsGALI), Olga Mikhailovna and me. The presidency was offered to Tvardovsky, which we fervently hoped he'd accept (his signature on Commission motions would carry weight). Tvardovsky agreed to become a member of the Commission but rejected the presidency, saying his busy schedule as editor of *Novy Mir* precluded it. We proposed Ehrenburg's and Paustovsky's candidacies, but the Writers' Management rejected them.

Berezko was an appropriate Commission Chairman. He knew Grossman well, dined out with him (Grossman was impressed by his manners in fine establishments, most notably at Derezemko), and appreciated and loved Grossman's literary talent. Once, we had all taken a trip to Yasnaya Polyana in a car belonging to one of Berezko's friends, and at the tomb of Tolstoy, Berezko said, "Now I feel as if I've kissed the edge of the Red Guard's flag." Grossman was derisive but good-humored about Berezko's literary work.

Initially, the Commission worked quite smoothly, even vigorously, especially considering we were dealing with the legacy of an arrested novel's author. What could we achieve? We could publish several of Grossman's short stories in magazines, his diary of the war years, and *Dobro Vam*. Alas, and sadly with the latter, only the version distorted by cuts. However, we couldn't achieve our primary goals; to publish a five-volume collected works and get *Life and Fate* withdrawn from Lubyanka and passed to TsGALI.

We decided to ask the Stalingrad (Volgograd) authorities

about naming a street or library after Grossman, a brave participant in the great battle. I was sent to Volgograd for this purpose. The Writers' Union apparently disapproved of the Commission's decision and refused to pay for this business trip. So I went on my own account and made an appointment with the Secretary of the Regional Committee for propaganda [Comrade] Nebenzy. He knew Grossman's work and promised to think about naming one of the newly opened libraries after the writer, but apparently, upon sage reflection and after wise consultation, the city fathers abandoned the idea.

Two deaths significantly damaged our committee, Tvardovsky's and Pismenny's. Their literary authority differed, but they were both equally decent men. I felt their absence particularly acutely one memorable day when we met for a session in a small room of the Writers' House. I'm not an intuitive man or a prophetic one; in all circumstances of life, I prefer to rely on facts, but that day, as we took our seats, the atmosphere from Berezko and Galin felt wrong. Finally, nervous and tentative, Berezko spoke, stammering even more than he usually did. "I can't make sense of why the writer-patriot I always considered Grossman to be, wrote that dirty, hostile story, *Everything Flows*, which has been published overseas and is being adulated by every low-life scum.

"I propose sending a letter to *Literaturnaya Gazeta* in the name of our entire Commission, in which we deplore with civic anger Grossman and the bourgeois scribblers, his extollers, and declare that they ask that our Commission be disbanded."

Galin joined Berezko's proposal and said he was also surprised; how could Grossman, who created the literary works so essential to our people, write such a slanderous story? He added, turning to me hopefully, "Maybe it wasn't Grossman who wrote it. Have you read it?" I answered with a question: "Have *you* read it? And you, Georgy Sergeyevich, have you read it?" Berezko and Galin kept silent. It was evident that they were deeply afraid.

I asked Berezko if he had received the instruction to write to *Literaturnaya Gazeta* about the dissolution of our Commission from the secretariat of the Moscow branch of the Writers' Union, in particular, the managing secretary Ilyin. It turned out there was no such instruction. Berezko and Galin were acting in anticipation; they were, as Platonov loved to call such people, "forestallers." "Raging at the enemies," as Berezko put it, "needs no command."

I said as Lebedev-Kumach teaches us, "Let our noble wrath / Seethe like waves,"[1] but I don't understand those who argue about a work without having read it. I said that the dissolution of our committee must come from the Secretariat, and until that happened, we would continue to do the job assigned to us by the Secretariat calmly by engaging in the publication and promotion of Grossman's literary heritage.

Quite unexpectedly, I was supported by the TsGALI employee Miralda Kozlova. Like many persons in this occupation, I had noticed that she always spoke sensibly and shunned demagogy. She said that the letter Berezko proposed to publish in *Literaturnaya Gazeta* would only benefit Grossman's enemies. We had to keep Grossman as a Soviet writer, not give him to his detractors. Let the people overseas believe that *Everything Flows* is the second part of the novel and continue to think so. Let them know nothing. Let them talk nonsense. We parted without taking any action, but after that, our meetings stopped. Berezko understood that he'd behaved badly. He ran into me once and asked, "Will you shake my hand?" I did. He was an insignificant, weak man; he could have been a decent man in a different society.

In due course, our Commission disbanded itself without a command from the authorities. Berezko and Galin died, and

---

1   +Vasily Lebedev-Kumach, *The Sacred War.*

I left the Writers' Union.[1] Grossman's works stopped being published. His name was rarely and reluctantly mentioned in the press. Readers' interest in his books faded, for readers read what they are given. And then came the news that *Life and Fate* had broken free after many years of incarceration; some of its chapters were printed in various journals. Would it be published fully? Years passed, but nothing was heard about a complete edition of the novel. The radio remained silent too. Knowledgeable people rationalized that the book was long, capitalism was capitalism, and a publisher who would take a risk on it would be hard to find. A project like that wouldn't yield the quick return on investment it would require. In addition, the reviewers might not like the novel; Grossman's name had no weight once it had lost its cachet in Russia.

What did I think? I felt bitter. The fate of Grossman's novel was related to his life and remained associated with his death. If such a great product as *Life and Fate* languished for decades in prison and didn't come out to readers in the West, then the West was worthy of tears and laughter but not of respect.

But I was wrong. I forgot Bulgakov's rule that the point is not to be surprised when trams run late but to allow for the surprise when they run to schedule. And to my surprise, the tram eventually started to run. Clever and gifted people who loved native literature with all their hearts, amid all the difficulties of their lives in exile, spared no effort in finding Grossman a 'selfish' publisher. And once they found him, despite unusual conditions and the need to use all conceivable means, this publisher prepared the book (which had been so grievously wounded on its long way from captivity to freedom) for publication.

The novel went to print, but the fact it wasn't spoken about

---

1   +In 1980, prompted by Inna Lisnyanskaya, Lipkin left The Writers' Union. *Metropole* was published, two less powerful contributers, Popov and Erofeev were censured. There had been a prior agreement where everyone would resign. Lipkin and Lisnyanskaya did.

on the radio shows how little its importance for Russia and Russian life was understood both at home and abroad. Anyway, I believed a reckoning approached and that everything would be resolved. To quote a wonderful verse from a minor Russian poet, "God was not tired; God was marching on"[1]. Despite long, sudden delays, the tram had finally arrived at our stop.

Of course, few people at home were on the tram's running board, and few have managed to read *Life and Fate*, but of those who have, no one, as far as I know, has been indifferent to its artistic power, beauty and grandeur. Everyone, be they man or woman, is moved by its Russian pain.

The West is the West, and translation to its national languages took a while, which is no surprise. The book's large – more than forty author's units – and the events it recounts, which occurred forty years ago, presented a risk to publishers.

But the book had been translated, and above all, into French, the language of eternal romance. They say in France, it became a bestseller. What elevating joy. Hearing this caused my pained heart to beat like a young man's, and the tears in my eyes were lit not by old age but by youth and excitement, hoping my Elysium friend could see and rejoice in the free flight of his creation.

I remember a wonderful place in his novel, full of poetic thought:

> Stalingrad's normalcy ended some months ago; schools, factories, dressmakers, nurseries, choral and theatre groups, movie houses, the police no longer function ... The flames had given birth to a new city, Stalingrad at war ...
>
> Every era has its own capital city, which embodies its spirit and soul. During a period of several months in the Second World War, Stalingrad was that capital ...

---

1   +Vladimir Benediktov (1807-1873).

An international capital's identity is not only due to its connection with the world's agriculture and manufacturing centers. An international capital's identity stems from the character of its soul. The soul of Stalingrad at war epitomizes freedom.

This is what we can say of Vasily Grossman's personal Stalingrad, that he was a firework that shone with multicolored fire, that his work saw freedom's victory. His tribesmen, Stendhal, Balzac, Flaubert, and Proust, were well aware of what a novel is. And it's worth listening to the French critics when in their articles they called *Life and Fate*, "the *War and Peace* of our time," "the great Russian novel," "A novel in the great Russian tradition," or "Titan at the heart of darkness." Petru Dumitriv's analysis was brilliant; he penetrated so profoundly into Grossman's very core that there is little point in raising minor discrepancies. Readers should get to know Dumitriv, who I assume is Catholic. Here are my rawest translations of some of what he wrote:

Grossman is an author and scientist at heart. There is a great and profound momentum in the spiritual life of a man of science, admiration for that tremendous inner world of matter, and at the same time for the way it mysteriously relates to the human spirit and the wonderous reality of the Universe.

Grossman stops at this junction. His characters do too. They're on the threshold of prayer. Just one step remains on the road to delight before the double secret, the secret of cognition of the bottomless rationality of the world and the mystery of God, which is the meaning of The Word, The Logos, and of God the Son Jesus Christ. Just one step is left, but Grossman doesn't know this.

Ikonnikov's manuscript is extremely important. It is Grossman's credo and philosophy, encapsulated as the underground movement of instinctive, blind and irresistible love and human kindness; "agape" in Koine Greek, "ahava" in Hebrew, "Love of God and Christ" in Christian theological terms. It is nothing but Love, [Ikonnikov asserts] the Love inherent in man from the first day of creation.

Grossman/Ikonnikov does not call this Love by name. Although he was a Jew and a Russian, he was blind, a Marxist-Leninist for too long ... Ignorant, prejudiced, and deaf to thought. He knew not Christ, nor even Buddha, and even less did he know their incarnation through the billions of people who followed them. However, I hope Christ will have mercy on me and forgive me if I dare to say that Grossman wasn't far from God's Kingdom.

These are the words of a man who did not know Grossman personally, had never met him but had a deeper understanding of him than many of those who saw and knew him. It is not easy, in either Russian or world literature, to find a writer whose moral ideal corresponds to his human traits and merges with them. We cannot say this even of Pushkin, or Tolstoy, the founder of one of Christianity's branches. In Russia, I find the complete fusion of human traits with the moral ideal of artistic creations in Korolenko[1], Chekhov, and Grossman. But the first two lived in times that seem rather wonderful to us today and so different to the present when simple everyday decency is so scarce that when we find it, we're amazed as if by a miracle.

Maybe that's why Grossman was considered grim, menacing, and sharp because he was not like his fellow writers, who, year after year, lost the human in themselves. Platonov was an exception, and it was this which led to his arduous destiny. No one obliged writers to follow Pushkin's example and write

---

1   + Vladimir Korolenko (1853-1921), Russian author and revolutionary.

letters to the prisoners in the depths of the Siberian mines.[1]

But how could these artists/writers demand publicly, in print, that their colleagues be strictly punished, excluded, condemned, imprisoned, or exiled? Nobody obliged academicians to follow Chekhov's example and protest against the persecution of their brothers. Why were they cowards? Why did they refuse to communicate with their persecuted brothers? Because they, these writers, these academicians lived dark lives, they did not have the light of life.

Three years after Grossman's death, I wrote a poem 'The Living':

Who are we? Bedouin whose tents
Are the gravestones which surround us
In Troyekurov cemetery
Where my only friend sleeps.
Above him, in a green open space,
Rise the joy and sorrow,
He built it as he argued with the inhuman,
In thousands of stories
Never having time to remove their scaffolding.
As though by his death, separating sin from sanctity,
He sleeps in the ground of Russian humility,
As patient as the earth itself.
And the word, creations of foundation,
Rises up again in the foliage,
The future breathes the past,
To re-embody it, because always,
The living live for the living,
And the dead only live for those who aren't alive.

---

1   +The Decembrists – Pushkin wrote a poem about The Decembrists in 1827 which was untitled and translated by Irina Zheleznova, "Deep in Siberia's mines let naught / Subdue your proud and patient spirit / Your crushing toll and lofty thought / Shall not be wasted – do not fear it."

Like the Romanian believer [Dumitriv], I ask God to forgive me when I say Grossman was a saint.

(1984)

EPILOGUE

I wrote the book that the reader has just read five years ago, but the past five years feel like an era. This newly open and democratic epoch has filled my life with a special light, and I can now clarify the mystery of Vasily Grossman's novel's publication.

I published a few rather harmless poems in the typed anthology *Metropol*. The authors of the anthology were brutally attacked by the Writers' Union. Two of the youngest, most vulnerable ones were excluded from the Union. In protest against the reprisals at the young authors, my wife, the poet Inna Lisnyanskaya and I resigned from the Writers' Union.

An avalanche of persecution rained down on us. We were ousted from the Literary Fund and expelled from the polyclinic (an illegal act insofar as it related to me: war veterans cannot be expelled from polyclinics). They not only stopped printing our translators' oeuvres but also our literary translations, which had once been highly praised in the press. There were other "delights" such as telephone threats, demands we leave the country, visits to our flat in our absences with traces deliberately left, and summonses to commissions where "competent persons" spoke to us.

In those circumstances, I couldn't say the things about Grossman's book that I'm going to say now.

As I said, Grossman offered *Life and Fate* to *Znamya* in the summer of 1960. Autumn came, and the editorial office hadn't responded. Once winter approached, Ekaterina Zabolotskaya and I raised the advantage with Grossman of having one type-written copy of the manuscript stored in a safe place. He gave us a long, careful, gloomy look and asked, "Are you both afraid that something bad will happen?"

I can't remember what Ekaterina said, but I said something like, "During the war, when Britain was bombed by the

Germans, Churchill said in Parliament, 'The worst is still to come.'" To which Grossman asked, "What do you suggest?"

"Give me a copy," I said.

So six months prior to its arrest, I had three light brown folders holding the three sections of *Life and Fate* in my possession. After considering the matter carefully, in all respects, I decided to hide the folders at a friendly house, far from the literary world.[1]

In his hospital room, shortly before he died, Grossman said to Ekaterina and me, "I don't want my coffin to lie at The Writers' Union. I want to be buried in Vostryakovskoye Jewish cemetery. I very much want my novel to be published, even if it's abroad."

His first two wishes were not met because Olga Mikhailovna wanted both her husband's civil funeral and burial to occur under the auspices of the Writers' Union. In addition, she wanted him buried in a prestigious cemetery. My friend's third wish I executed, though not immediately.

It was only at the end of 1974 that I took a firm decision to ask Vladimir Nikolayevich Voinovich to help me publish Grossman's novel. I chose Voinovich because we were friends and neighbors, and I knew he had experience of being published abroad.

Voinovich agreed readily. Inna Lisnyanskaya took the three folders to Voinovich as it seemed unwise to do so myself. Voinovich tried to microfilm the typescript, but his first attempt was unsuccessful. However, Voinovich was persistent in all things and made repeated attempts. I later learned that he'd enlisted Elena Bonner's and Andrei Sakharov's assistance to allow the novel to escape from bondage.

Foreign publishers of Russian literature refused to publish *Life and Fate* for five years. I was told they didn't think a novel about World War Two would interest their current readers and

---

1   +The folders were hidden in the attic of Inna's daughter and son law, Lena and Sergei Makarov's Moscow's flat.

that Stalin's camps had already been described well enough by Solzhenitsyn. Finally, the owner of the Swiss non-profit publishing house L'Age d'Homme published a small edition of the novel in Russian.

When it was first published abroad, words, phrases, and even whole pages were missing. This was solely due to the imperfect photography; in no case did these omissions relate to the novel's ideological content.

Eventually, the novel attracted the attention of European language translators and publishers. After the book's initial French champions and its unprecedented success, there were translations into English, German, and, I believe, Spanish.

When he read the novel, the editor of *Oktyabr [October]*, Anatoly Ananyev, saw its merit and, acting with extraordinary courage and literary audacity, printed it in his journal. Ananyev's action led to *Life and Fate* becoming a national treasure in the eyes of a broad mass of Soviet readers.

A new Commission for Vasily Grossman's Literary Heritage has been formed, of which I'm a member. In this capacity, I have given all three folders of Grossman's manuscript to Ananyev, the Commission's Chairman. Russia's readers will now be able to enjoy their favorite novel in its entirety.

Only last year, on December 12th [1988], while we in the Grossman coterie celebrated his birthday, I learned for the first time that Grossman had given a draft of the novel to a friend I'd met through him, Vyacheslav Loboda. I don't know how or when he did that, Grossman wisely never told me he had done so. In those days, it was better that people knew only what they needed to know. I saw Loboda's draft; it was a heavily corrected typescript, and the small handwriting in which it was corrected was familiar. I compared its pages to those of the clean typescript I'd saved. Loboda's draft, as corrected, proved to be the final copy of Grossman's manuscript.

(September 1st 1989)

BIBLIOGRAPHY OF LIPKIN'S WORK

Poetry:

Ochevidets [Eyewitness: poems of various years]; Elista: Kalmyk Book Publishers, 1967; 2nd Edition, 1974.

Vechnyi Den' [Eternal Day]; Moscow: Sovetsky Pisatel', 1975.

Volia [Free Will]; selected by Joseph Brodsky. Ann Arbor: Ardis, 1981; Moscow: O.G.I., 2003.

Kochevoi Ogon' [A Nomadic Flame]; Ann Arbor: Ardis, 1984.

Kartiny i golosa [Pictures and Voices]; London: Overseas Publications Interchange, 1986.

Lira. Stikhi Raznyh Let [Lyre. Verses of Various Years]; Moscow: Pravda, 1989.

Lunnyi Svet. Stikhotvoreniya i Poemy [Moonlight. Verses and Poems]; Moscow: Sovremennik, 1991.

Pis'mena. Stikhotvoreniya i Poemy [Letters. Verses and Poems]; Moscow: Khudozhestvennaia Literatura, 1991.

Pered Zakhodom Solntsa. Stikhi i Perevody [Before the Sunset. Verses and Translations]; Paris-Moscow-New York: Tretya Volna, 1995.

Posokh [Shepherd's Crook]. Moscow: CheRo, 1997.

Sobranie sochinenia v 4-kh tomakh [Collected works in 4 volumes]; Moscow: Vagrius, 1998.

Sem' desiatiletii [Seven Decades]; Moscow: Vozvrashchenie, 2000.

Vmeste. Stikhi [Together, Verses]; (Together with Inna Lisnyanskaya). Moscow: Grail, Russkiy put', 2000.

Ochevidets [Eyewitness: selected poems]; Compiled by Inna Lisnyanskaya. Moscow: Vremia, 2008.

Prose:

The Stalingrad Ship (stories), 1943

Decade (first novel), 1983

Stalingrad of Vasily Grossman, 1984

Life and Fate of Vasily Grossman. Farewell (With Anna Berzer), 1990

The Flaming Coal. Sketches and Discourses, 1991

The Second Road (memoirs), 1995

Blazing Fire (sketches and observations about Georgii Shengeli), 1995

Kvadriga (short fiction and memoirs), 1997

Examples of Translations by Lipkin:

Abkhaz

Bagrat Shikuba, Moi zemlyaki [My Compatriots, a poem]; transl. from Abkhaz by S. Lipkin and Ya. Kozlovsky. Moscow, 1967.

Akkadian

Gilgamesh; verse adaptation by Semyon Lipkin; afterword by Vyacheslav V. Ivanov. St Petersburg: Pushkin Fund, 2001.

Buryat

Geser [Geser, Buryat Heroic Epos]; Moscow: Khudozhestvennaia Literatura, 1968

Derzhava rannikh zhavoronkov. Povest po motivam bury-atskogo eposa [The State of Early Skylarks. A novella on the Motives of Buryat Epos]; a children's version by S. Lipkin. Moscow: Detgiz, 1968.

Dagestani

Dagestanskie liriki [*Dagestani Lyric Poets*]; translations by S.I. Lipkin and others. Leningrad: Sovetsky Pisatel', 1961.

Kabardian

Shogentsukov, Ali. Poemy [*Poems*]; translated from Kabardian by Semyon Lipkin. Moscow: Sovetsky Pisatel', 1949.

Narty [*Narts, Kabardian Epos*]; translated by Semyon Lipkin. Moscow: Khudozhestvennaia Literatura, 1951.

Kabardinskaia epicheskaya poezia [*Kabardian Epic Poetry*]; selected translations. Nal'chik, 1956.

Debet Zlatolikii i ego druzia: Balkaro-Karachaev nartskii epos [*Debet Goldenface and his friends: Karachai-Balkar Nart epic*]; translated by S. Lipkin. Nal'chik: Elbrus, 1973.

Kalmyk

Prikliyucheniya bogatyrya Samshura, prozvannogo Lotosom [*Adventures of Hero Shamshur, Nicknamed Lotus*], a children's adaptation of the Kalmyk epic story by Semyon Lipkin. Moscow: Detgiz, 1958.

Dzhangar: Kalmytski narodny epos [*Djangar: Kalmyk national epic*]; translated by Semyon Lipkin. Elista: Kalmyk Book Publishers, 1971, repr. 1977.

Dzhangar: Kalmytski narodny epos; novye pesni [*Djangar: Kalmyk national epic; new songs*]; poetic translations realised by V N Eremenko, S.I. Lipkin, Yu. M. Neiman. Elista: Kalmyk Book Publishers, 1990.

Kirghiz

Kirgizskii narodnyi epos "Manas" [*Kirghiz Folk Epos Manas*], transl. Semyon Lipkin and Mark Tarlovsky. Moscow: Khudozhestvennaia Literatura, 1941.

Poety Kirgizii: Stikhi 1941–1944 [*Kirghiz Poets: Verses 1941–1944*]; translated under the editorship of S. Lipkin. Moscow: Sovetskiy Pisatel', 1946.

Manas Velikodushny: povest [Manas the Magnanimous: a novella]; (version by S. Lipkin). Leningrad, 1947.

Manas: epizody iz kirgizskogo narodnogo eposa [*Manas: episodes from the Kirghiz national epic*]; translated by S. Lipkin and L. Penkovski. Moscow: Khudozhestvennaia Literatura, 1960.

Manas Velikodushny. Povest' o drevnikh kirghizskikh geroyakh [*Manas the Magnanimous: a Story about Ancient Kirghiz Heroes*]; Riga: Polaris, 1995.

Sanskrit

Mahabharata (Indian epic). In: series Biblioteka vsemirnoi literatury, vol.2, translated from Sanskrit by S. Lipkin. Moscow: Khudozhestvennaia Literatura, 1969.

Tatar

Poety Tatarii, 1941–1944 [*Poets of Tataria, 1941–1944*]; edited by A. Erikeeva and S. Lipkin. Moscow: Sovetsky Pisatel', 1945.

Poeziya Sovetskoi Tatarii: Sbornik sostavlen Soiuzom Sovetskikh Pisatelei Tatarskoi ASSR [*Poetry of Soviet Tataria: Collection compiled by the Union of Soviet Tatar Writers*]; editor S.I. Lipkin [translations by various hands].Moscow: Khudozhestvennaia Literatura, 1955.

Idegei: tatarskii narodnyi epos [*Idegei: Tatar national epic*]; translated by Semyon Lipkin. Kazan': Tatar Book Publishers, 1990.

Tadjik-Farsi

Firdawsi. Skazanie o Bakhrame Chubine [*Epos about Bakhram*

Chubin]; a fragment from poem Shāhnāmah translated from Tadjik-Farsi by S. Lipkin. Stalinabad [Dushanbe]: Tadzhikgosizdat, 1952.

Izbrannoe [*Selections*]; translated from Tadjik-Farsi by V. Levik and S. Lipkin. Moscow, 1957.

Firdawsi. Poėmy iz Shakh-namė [*Poems from Shāhnāmah*]; in translation by S. Lipkin. Stalinabad [Dushanbe]: Tadzhikgosizdat, 1959.

Stranitsy Tadzhikskoy Poezii [*Pages of Tadjik Poetry*]; ed. S. Lipkin, Stalinabad [Dushanbe]: Tadzikgosizdat, 1961.

Rudaki, stikhi [*Rudaki, verses*]; transl. S. Lipkin and V. Levik, ed. I. Braginsky. Moscow: Nauka, 1964.

Tetrad' bytiia [*Book of Life*]; Poetry in Tadjik dialect with Russian by Semyon Lipkin. Lipkin. Dushanbe: Irfon, 1977.

Uzbek

Khamid Alimdzhan. Oigul i Bakhtiyor [*Oigul i Bakhtiyor*]; Tashkent: Goslitizdat UzSSR, 1948.

Lutfi. Gul I Navruz [*Gul and Navruz, a poem*]; transl. S.Lipkin. Tashkent: Goslitizdat UzSSR, 1959.

Navoi, Leili i Medzhnun [*Leili and Medjnun*]; poem translated from Uzbek by Semyon Lipkin. Moscow: Goslitizdat, 1945; Moscow: Detgiz, 1948; Tashkent: Khudozhestvennaia Literatura, 1957; (In: A Navoi. *Poėmy* [*Poems*].), Moscow: Khudozhestvennaia Literatura, 1972.

Navoi, Sem' Planet [*Seven Planets*]; poem translated from Uzbek by Semyon Lipkin. Tashkent, 1948; Moscow, 1954; (In: A. Navoi. Poemy [*Poems*].); Moscow: Khudozhestvennaia Literatura, 1972.

Golosa Shesti Stoletii [*Voices of Six Centuries*]; selected translations from Uzbek. Tashkent, 1960.

Tsarevna iz goroda T'my [*Princess from the City of Darkness*];

children's story by S. Lipkin based on Uzbek tales. Moscow: Detgiz, 1961.

Slovo i Kamen [*Word and Stone*]; selected translations from Uzbek poetry by S. Lipkin, Tashkent: Gafur Gulyam Publ., 1977.

Mixed Language Anthologies:

Stroki Mudrykh [*Lines of the Wise Ones*]; coll. translations by S. Lipkin,Moscow: Sovetskiy Pisatel', 1961.

O bogatyriakh, umeltsakh i volshebnikhakh [*On Heroes, Craftsmen and Wizards*]; 3 novellas on Caucasian folklore motives, children's adaptation by S. Lipkin. Moscow: Detgiz, 1963.

Zolotaya zep' [*The Golden Chain: Eastern Poems*]; translated from Abkhaz, Tadzhik-Farsi, old-Uzbek, etc. Moscow: Detgiz, 1970.

Dalekie i Blizkie: Stikhi zarubezhnykh poetov v perevode [*Far and Near: Verses by foreign poets in translation*]; translators: Vera Markova, Semyon Lipkin, Aleksandr Gitovich. Moscow: Progress, 1978.

Bibliography of Translations of Lipkin's Work

English translations of Lipkin's work:

One poem translated by Yvonne Green, one poem translated by Robert Chandler, in *The Penguin Book of Russian Poetry* by Robert Chandler, Boris Drayluk and Irina Mashinski, Penguin Classics 2015.

Six poems translated by Yvonne Green, 2 poems translated by Daniel Weissbort, in *Cardinal Points*, www.stosvet.net/12/green, 2011

Two poems translated by Amelia Glaser, in *An Anthology of Jewish-Russian Literature Volume 2 1953-2001* edited by Maxim D Shrayer, M E Sharpe Inc, 2007.

Four poems translated by Albert C. Todd, in *Twentieth Century Russian Poetry*, selected with an introduction by Yevgeny Yevtushenko, edited by Albert C. Todd and Max Hayward, with Daniel Weissbort. New York: Doubleday; London: Fourth Estate, 1993.

French translations of Lipkin's work:

Le Destin De Vassili Grossman translated by Alexis Berelowitch, L'Age d'Homme, Lausanne, 1990.

SUGGESTED FURTHER READING BY ABIGAIL HAYTON

These memoirs deal with probably the most turbulent, and definitely the bloodiest, period in human history about which countless works have been written, both philosophical and historical. Here we've seen the perspective of a Soviet writer who's both a dissident and a servant of the regime which defined his life and work. The construction of the USSR is beautifully and readably detailed in Orlando Figes's *A People's Tragedy: The Russian Revolution 1891–1924.*[1] The Russian Civil War, the second stage of the Revolution and the process by which its course was set is given its most comprehensive review yet, from a trans-Imperial perspective, particularly important in view of Lipkin's work as a translator, in Jonathan Smele's *The 'Russian' Civil Wars 1916–1926: Ten Years that Shook the World.*[2] Stalin's seizure of power, and the regime he created, or shaped, is well documented: a biography which informatively juxtaposes the private Stalin with the public *Vozhd* is Simon Sebag-Montefiore's *Stalin: The Court of the Red Tsar.*[3] The most important work on Stalin's terror published to date is Robert Conquest's *The Great Terror: A Reassessment.*[4] Martin Amis's *Koba the Dread* vivifies the collusion of Western intellectuals.[5] Donald Rayfield's *Stalin and his Hangmen* is also worth consulting for its exploration of Stalin's policy of terror and those who carried it out.[6] This perspective on Soviet Russia is of vital importance for an understanding of the work here

---

1 *A People's Tragedy: The Russian Revolution 1891-1924* (Pimlico, 1997).
2 *The 'Russian' Civil Wars 1916-1926: Ten Years that Shook the World* (C Hurst & Co, 2015).
3 *Stalin: The Court of the Red Tsar* (Phoenix, 2012).
4 *The Great Terror: A Reassessment* (Pimlico, 2008).
5 *Koba the Dread* (Vintage, 2003).
6 *Stalin and his Hangmen: an Authoritative Portrait of a Tyrant and those who Served Him* (Penguin, 2005).

presented. For an assessment of the cultural and personal implications of the Stalinist regime see Orlando Figes's *The Whisperers: Private Life in Stalin's Russia.*[1]

Lipkin's memoirs are an important testament (*Kvadriga*) to the lives and works of the USSR's literary elite. For a broader overview of the USSR's literary climate, see Solomon Volkov's *Magical Chorus.*[2] For an historical overview, see Orlando Figes's *Natasha's Dance* which provides an analysis of Russian cultural history, placing the writers of the USSR within the context of their national literary and artistic histories.[3] An analysis of the twentieth century in Russian philosophy has been provided by Mikhail Epstein, who treats contemporary Russian thought as part of a broader scheme of Russian intellectual history, observing philosophical continuities from Tsarism to Communism. His in-depth analysis is particularly potent given his probing of the philosophical implications of the worldviews referred to in Lipkin's memoir, particularly concerning the relation of the artist to regime and the perilous relationship between 'filosofia' and politics.[4] Robert Chandler's *The Penguin Book of Russian Poetry* sheds further light on the particular contribution of poetry to this vitally important, though perhaps underrepresented, period in Russian intellectual history.[5]

Within the work, Lipkin frequently references both contemporary works and nineteenth-century classics. His writing assumes an intimacy with Russian and indeed, European, literature as a whole. Some knowledge of these works is essential to those who would wish to see the USSR through his eyes.

1 *The Whisperers: Private Life in Stalin's Russia (Penguin, 2008).*
2 *Magical Chorus* (Vintage, 2009).
3 *Natasha's Dance (Penguin, 2003).*
4 'The Phoenix of Philosophy: On the Meaning and Significance of Contemporary Russian Thought', in *Symposium: A Journal of Russian Thought (1996)*, Vol. 1, pp. 35-74. http://www.emory.edu/INTELNET/ar_phoenix_philosophy.html
5 *The Penguin Book of Russian Poetry* (Penguin, 2015).

Lermontov, Tolstoy and Pushkin are key points of reference for him. As the translation here presented focuses on the story of Grossman's *Life and Fate*, that is an essential point of reference.[1] Also of note is Grossman's *An Armenian Sketchbook*, the writing of which has been discussed here.[2] For Grossman's journalistic writing, see *A Writer at War*, a selection of his extracts from that period, translated by Antony Beevor.[3] Much of Lipkin's story of the life of Grossman is corroborated by Anna Berzer's *Proshchanie* [*Farewell*], published in Moscow in 1990.[4]

Lipkin is best known in Russia for his poetry, which is currently being made available to readers of the English language by this book's translators: *After Semyon Izrailevich Lipkin* was published by Smith|Doorstop in 2011. Daniel Weissbort has published his own translations of Lipkin's 'Before May' and 'The Carriage' online.[5] Lipkin's novel *A Resident Remembers* has been made available in English by the translator, Arch Tait.[6] Inna Lisnyanskaya, Lipkin's wife, mentioned briefly here – also well-known in her native country, and increasingly revered in the Anglophone world – has been translated by Daniel Weissbort, who has produced a collection of her works entitled *Far From Sodom*.[7]

Even in the English-speaking world, Lipkin's memoir *Kvadriga* has long been cited as an important source for those writing on Soviet literature. Yuri Leving's 2009 article in *The Slavic and East European Journal* entitled 'Whose is

---

1 *Life and Fate* (Vintage, 2006).
2 *An Armenian Sketchbook* (MacLehose Press, 2013).
3 *A Writer at War: Vasily Grossman with the Red Army 1941–1945* (Pimlico, 2006).
4 *Proshchanie [Farewell]* (Moscow: Kniga, 1990).
5 'Cardinal Points Literary Journal' http://www.stosvet.net/12/weissbort/index3.html, [accessed: 17.09. 14]
6 *Winners and Others, Glas New Russian Writing 7 (1994), pp. 43–55.*
7 *Far from Sodom* (Ark, 2005).

the Seal-Ring? Kliuev's Subtexts in Mandelstam's Poem 'Give Tiutchev a Dragonfly", uses Lipkin to bring to light details of the relationship between Mandelstam and Kliuev.[1] Frequent references to *Kvadriga* are made by John Garrard in his article on Grossman's *Everything Flows*, which was published in *The Slavic and East European Journal* of Summer 1994.[2] Nienke Van der Heide's 2008 work on the cultural life of Kyrgyzstan contains some details of his role as translator and the interactions of Lipkin with the authorities which this entailed: *Kvadriga*, is frequently quoted from.[3] The story in the first extract about Ahkmatovas's summoning of Lipkin to share her outrage at a suggestion in a French magazine that she had been abandoned by her husband, Lev Gumilyev, is corroborated by Kornei Chukovsky's diaries of that year (1967).[4]

Lipkin's memories of Mandelstam are also relied upon in Donald Loewen's *The Most Dangerous Art*, a fascinating work on the relationship between poetry and authority in the USSR, which references many of the writers and incidents recalled by Lipkin in *Kvadriga*.[5] Its primary subjects are Mandelstam, Tsevetaeva and Pasternak. In Robert Chandler's introduction to his most recent translation of Vasily Grossman, *An Armenian Sketchbook*, *Kvadriga* is referenced in relation to Grossman's health at the time of his travels in Armenia.[6] Lipkin is also called upon as a witness to the story of Grossman and Olga Guber in Chandler's introduction to his translation of *Life and Fate*. The same piece references his account in several

---

1 *The Slavic and East European Journal*, Vol. 53, No. 1 (Spring, 2009), pp41-64, (p49).
2 'The Original Manuscript of Forever Flowing: Grossman's Autopsy of the New Soviet Man', *TSEEJ*, Vol. 53, No. 2 (Summer, 1994), pp. 271-289.
3 *Spirited Performance: The Manas Epic and Society in Kyrgyzstan* (2008), pp183-189.
4 *Diary 1901-1969* (Yale University Press, 2005) p524.
5 *The Most Dangerous Art: Poetry, Politics and Autobiography after the Russian Revolution* (Lexington Books, 2008), pp42-43.
6 *An Armenian Sketchbook* (MacLehose Press, 2013), p11.

places as an authority on Grossman's health in the latter part of his life, and his key role in the preservation of the precious manuscript.[1] In his translation of *Everything Flows* (sometimes referred to as "Forever Flowing"), Robert Chandler includes an afterword by Yekaterina Grossman, Grossman's daughter, which describes Grossman and Lipkin sitting together for many hours, listening to the stories of the man who was to become 'Romashkin' in that novel.[2]

The journey of *Life and Fate* can be paralleled with that other great work of Soviet fiction to be published initially in the West and then in Russia, Pasternak's *Dr Zhivago*. Peter Finn and Petra Couvee's recent work on the 'Zhivago Affair' uses *Kvadriga* as a source.[3] Another recent work on The Zhivago Affair, Paolo Mancosu's *Inside the Zhivago Storm* is also worth consulting, for an insider's view of the journey of this novel from conception to publication, originally in Italy in 1957.[4]

In Solomon Volkov's *Conversations with Joseph Brodsky*, he recalls Brodsky's admiration for Lipkin, whom he saw as 'a remarkable poet', the mouthpiece for Russia's *belles lettres* during the war years, thus saving 'our national reputation'.[5] It was, in fact, on Brodsky's initiative that Lipkin's *Volia* was published in 1981.[6] This collection was reviewed by Victoria A Woodbury in *World Literature Today*.[7]

The 'Metropol Affair', referred to towards the end of the extract here presented, is described in detail by Vassily

---

1 'Introduction' in *Life and Fate*, Vasily Grossman (Vintage, 2006).

2 'Afterword' in *Everything Flows*, Vasily Grossman (Vintage, 2011), pp. 289-290

3 *The Zhivago Affair: The Kremlin, the CIA and the Battle over a Forbidden Book* (Random House, 2014).

4 *Inside the Zhivago Storm: The Editorial Adventures of Pasternak's Masterpiece* (Feltrineli, 2014).

5 *Conversations with Joseph Brodsky: A Poet's Journey Through the Twentieth Century*, p. 50.

6 *Volya* (Ann Arbor, 1981).

7 'Volja by Semën Lipkin; Iosif Brodskij', *World Literature Today*, Vol. 56, No. 1 (Winter 1982), pp. 133-134.

Aksyonov in his article of that name, written for *The Wilson Quarterly* in 1982.[1] It represents a tragic reassertion of 'Socialist Realism', twenty-five years after the death of Stalin, demonstrating the Soviet ideal, by its very nature, to be an enemy of the arts, which Lipkin saw, in its purest form, to be the pursuit of truth.[2] Lipkin refers to his participation in the *Metropol* journal as the contribution of "a few, rather harmless poems", but his participation in the affair, and subsequent resignation from the Writers' Union, alongside his wife, Inna, sounded, for many, the death knell of Socialist Realism.[3] This episode is also recalled in *Inside the Soviet Writers' Union* by John Gordon Garrard and Carol Garrard and Robert Porter's *Russia's Alternative Prose*[4], which looks at the fate of Russian literature, post Gorbachev and is an important account of this period. For a contemporary Western review of *Metropol*, see *The Slavic and Eastern European Journal* of spring, 1984, where it was assessed by Ronald E Peterson.[5]

This list reflects my personal preferences and is not intended to be exhaustive, but hopefully it provides a starting point for the interested reader, both scholarly and otherwise, to plunge further into the world of Semyon Izraelivch Lipkin, and the literary culture he gives us an insider's view of in his memoirs.

---

1 'The Metropol Affair', *The Wilson Quarterly* (1976-), Vol. 6, No. 5, Special Issue (1982), pp. 152-159.

2 *Kvadriga* (2015)

3 *Kvadriga* (2015)

4 *Inside the Soviet Writers' Union* (Free Press, 1990), p. 189: *Russia's Alternative Prose* (Berg, 1994).

5 'Metropol: Literary Almanac by Vasily Aksyonov; Victor Yerofeyev; Fazil Iksander; Andrei Bitov; Yevgeny Popov; Christina Dodds-Ega; Martin Horwitz; Boris Jakim; Vladimir Lunis; Carl Proffer; Barry Rubin; George Saunders; H William Tjalsma', *TSEEJ*, Vol. 28, No. 1 (Spring, 1984), pp 128-130.

INDEX OF NAMES REFERRED TO IN THESE PAGES

INDEX OF NAMES REFERRED TO IN THESE PAGES

Printed in Great Britain
by Amazon

20363811R00127